Advance Praise

He's Just Not Your Type (and that's a good thing):

"In terms of love and relationships, Andrea Syrtash has 'been there' and 'done that' and has mastered the dating game, in part by throwing away the rules and proving it's not a game at all, but rather a journey that needs to be undertaken with exuberance, honesty, and an appetite for the unexpected. Her voice is fresh, funny, and relatable, and the advice in *He's Just Not Your Type* is spot-on. I've already given my copy to my single cousin!"
—Ian Kerner, best-selling author of
She Comes First and *Be Honest, You're Not That Into Him Either*

"Andrea Syrtash offers some of the most practical approaches to dating that I've ever seen. She takes the guesswork out of it and teaches you how to lead with your heart. When I read her advice, 'Date the person, not the potential,' it made me smile. Get her book today . . . and you'll be smiling, too!"
—Lisa Nichols, best-selling author of
No Matter What! and featured teacher in *The Secret*

"As someone who married her nontype, I can confidently say that Andrea nailed the process of how to mindfully date men who recognize and encourage you to be the best version of yourself—and never (okay, rarely) look back on the chumps who came before."
—Kristina Grish, author of *The Joy of Text* and *Boy Vey!*

"Written from a place of deep caring and experience, Syrtash points out that what we think we want, and what's really good for us, are often two different things. If this wise book doesn't jolt you out of your old, broken dating patterns, nothing else will."
—Evan Marc Katz, dating coach and coauthor of *Why You're Still Single*

"Confused by your 'bad luck' in dating? Then you're lucky to have found this book! Syrtash explains in a fun and entertaining way how you developed your dating patterns—then inspires you to think differently, snagging you different (and happier!) dating results!"
—Karen Salmansohn, author of *Prince Harming Syndrome*

"Finally, *real* love lessons for single women without any 'rules'! Kudos to Andrea for teaching us right from wrong and how not to settle for Mr. Maybe."
—Sherri Langburt, founder of SingleEdition.com

HE'S JUST NOT YOUR TYPE

(AND THAT'S A GOOD THING)

HOW TO FIND LOVE
WHERE YOU LEAST EXPECT IT

ANDREA SYRTASH

RODALE

Rodale books may be purchased for business or promotional use or for special sales. For information, please write to: Special Markets Department, Rodale Inc., 733 Third Avenue, New York, NY 10017.

Printed in the United States of America

Rodale Inc. makes every effort to use acid-free ♾, recycled paper ♻.

Book design by Joanna Williams

Library of Congress Cataloging-in-Publication Data
Syrtash, Andrea.
    He's just not your type (and that's a good thing) : how to find love where you least expect it / Andrea Syrtash.
        p.   cm.
    ISBN-13: 978–1–60529–673–9 paperback
    ISBN-10: 1–60529–673–2 paperback
    1. Mate selection. 2. Dating (Social customs) 3. Single women. I. Title.
HQ801.S98 2010
646.7'7–dc22   2010001157

Distributed to the trade by Macmillan

2 4 6 8 10 9 7 5 3 1 paperback

To fabulous single women everywhere who should never feel they have to settle in order to settle down.

"I'm seeing someone . . . sort of. It's ridiculous—he's so-o-o not my type. He's bald. And short. And he talks with his mouth full . . . and . . . it's the best sex of my life. . . . I think I might really like him."

—Charlotte York, from Sex and the City

Contents

Prologue

I Didn't Mean to Fall in Love with Him…

It was September 2005 when I realized I had accidentally fallen in love with Michael.

I was horrified. I wanted to be one of those women who, upon getting engaged, tells her friends, "I *knew* from the first moment I saw him that he was the one!" The day I realized that I wanted to spend the rest of my life with my longtime friend and neighbor, I was terrified.

Michael was the fun guy in the neighborhood. He had more chutzpah than anyone I had ever met. (He would walk into our house, put on my sister's slippers, and start making eggs . . . without even saying hello!) Michael was a teacher, an improv actor, and a drummer. His favorite T-shirt, which he wore often, was vintage—but not in a hipster kind of way. It was paper thin and displayed a photo of Michael's prepubescent face framed by a WANTED sign with the caption "Roger's Bar Mitzvah. December 1990." I believe it had a hole in the left armpit.

This was not the guy I'd envisioned bringing home to Dad and certainly not the guy I envisioned ever *being* a dad. If anything, Michael was boyfriend (not husband!) material—for someone else.

Dating before Michael

Over the years, I had dated several "perfect" men who made good money, treated me well, and knew exactly the right thing to say at social functions. These men were often a little older than me and usually a lot more stable. Their qualities looked great on paper and satisfied my checklist of "good husband material." They were ready for marriage, but I always delayed the decision with excuses like "I think we should just date another year. What's the rush?"

Friends jokingly dubbed me "the Runaway Bride," since each time I was close to a marriage proposal from a wonderful catch, I took off. When I broke up with one such boyfriend, he called me out. "You'll never settle down!" he said. "You have commitment problems. Do you know how many women would be happy to marry me?"

He was right. While most women I knew fantasized about weddings with guys like him, I dreamed up escape routes.

I began to realize that not only was I on a different page from my boyfriends, but I was in another chapter—or maybe even a different book. After the end of yet another chapter, I decided to move back to my sister's house in Toronto and start practicing what I preached. After all, I'd been an advice writer for almost a decade, instructing people to follow their passions, live their best lives, and stay true to themselves. I coached people in dating and told them that in order to find love, they had to be *open* to possibility and replace the word *should* with *want* (more on that later). Given the state of my love life, I felt like a fraud.

So I made a conscious decision to focus on my dating pattern. We all have one. I realized that my head dominated my heart and that I hadn't been giving enough attention to my feelings. I had spent time carefully analyzing the details of my relationships while completely ignoring my instincts. With this shift in my perspective, I also realized that perhaps the men I'd always thought of as my "type" were not the people with whom I would find long-term love and happiness.

I thought about the qualities that were most important to me in a mate. I realized I wanted to be with a guy who made me laugh and who was emotionally intelligent and spiritually connected. I wanted to be with a man who deeply understood and inspired me, like a soul mate. I did not know what he would look like, but I knew how I wanted to *feel* around him. For the first time, I became less concerned with who this man was and more concerned with who I would be with him.

I used to think I had a problem committing to a relationship. It never occurred to me that the problem wasn't some inherent flaw in me; it was in the choices I was making, the men I was choosing to date. I've talked to so many women who are in the same position, even if they don't realize it. For example, I've listened to clients confess that they've had little success in love, even though they admit that the men they date warn them early on that they're not ready for a long-term commitment. Women date these men in the hope that they will change their minds (or that their minds can be changed), but dating a man for his potential, and not for the person he is today, is usually a path to heartache.

I've talked to other women who use a mental checklist full of external criteria (as I had done) to determine their ideal mate, focusing more on earning potential and college degrees than emotional and physical compatibility. They date the same kinds of men over and over, moving from one failed relationship to the next. In other words, they get caught up in a dating pattern that is simply not working. If you are familiar with Einstein's definition of insanity—doing the same thing over and over and expecting different results—this behavior could classify a person as insane.

I do not believe in bad luck in dating—just bad choices.

Throughout this book, you can expect to be challenged, guided, supported, and entertained. I will ask you tough questions, make you dig deep, and assign exercises and dating homework (trust me, that's the fun part). As you gain self-awareness, you will learn to take responsibility for your role in your dating pattern. And as you begin to apply what you've learned about yourself, your love life will undoubtedly improve. Most important, you will learn to break self-defeating patterns and create a new recipe for happiness.

Along the way, I'll share the true stories of clients and friends who found lasting happiness with their own "nontypes" (NTs), including men who made less money, were not a physical "match," were of a different faith, lived far away, were divorced, or otherwise possessed characteristics that might have immediately ruled them out as potential dates.

NTs come in many different packages, and they are not always so extreme, but they may challenge your long-held mental picture of your future mate. If you have ever dreamed about someone but ignored those feelings because you did not think you should pursue a relationship with someone like him, think again.

So—what did I do when I realized I had fallen for my neighbor? I asked him to join me for dinner at our favorite local Mexican dive. When he picked me up, I was more nervous than I had been on a date in years. We sat down at the table, and I said, like a rambling fool, "I don't know where you are in your life . . . or if you see me this way . . . or if you even want to try dating me . . . or if you think that would ruin the friendship, but I want to try dating you."

And just like the Hollywood ending I had been searching for all along, Michael said, with salsa on his chin, "I feel the same way."

It took years of dating all kinds of "perfect" men for me to realize that Michael *was* perfect . . . for me.

Part I

Think Outside the Box(ers)

I

Don't "Should" All Over Yourself

I know we haven't yet officially met, but if you are single and questioning your ability to find a successful romantic relationship or attract a mate, let me reassure you that there is nothing wrong with you. You do not have bad luck in dating. You are not destined for a lifetime of spending your weekends on dates with your friends, their husbands . . . and their babies.

In fact, you are hardly alone. We are living in an era with more singles than ever before. The US Census Bureau recognizes close to 100 million Americans who are unmarried. We are taking longer to settle down because, frankly, we do not want to settle. Women today are hoping to marry—not simply to procreate or to honor our families—but for a radical and modern reason: love.

By this point in your life, I'm sure you've met men who seem perfectly fine but with whom you're not interested in pursuing a relationship. In some ways, it would be easier if you could just marry one of these "good enough" men. But you want a real connection, and you don't want to compromise your standards.

You may have picked up this book because family members have labeled your dating habits ("Too picky"), or concerned friends want you to couple up and settle down ("You're a great catch!"), or mere acquaintances remind you that time is of the essence ("You're not getting any younger!"). Perhaps you have even assigned yourself a label ("Unlucky in love"). But I promise, you are okay. You just haven't dated *the right kind of person for you.*

I often hear people mention that they have lost hope because their dates and relationships never seem to work out. Here's a simple truth: Most dating scenarios are destined to fail! Until you find the person you want to marry, every relationship will be *unsuccessful.*

The important piece is that when a series of dates with one person or a relationship does not work out, you can walk away from it with new insights on *how you want to be* and *who you want to be with* in your next relationship.

That's the good news. And now for the not-so-good news (I hate to be a pessimist).

You may repeat your dating pattern for many more years—and stay single when you'd rather not be—if you do not start making conscious changes and looking at your choices.

Before I delve into my crazy (but you'll see very logical) premise about dating your nontypes, I will ask you to commit to examining your relationship pattern. And I believe the first step in creating this paradigm shift starts with making a shift in your language.

You may be thinking, "I'm reading this book for tips on how to find a good relationship, not to get language lessons!" But trust me on this: The messages we tell ourselves and the ideas that seep into our minds from parents, friends, and society do affect our love lives.

Stop Shoulding All Over Yourself

I *shouldn't* be so picky. I *should* be with (fill in name of a guy you know who doesn't inspire or excite you but is perfectly nice): He makes decent money and comes from a good family. I'd have a nice life with him.

I *should* be having babies by now. Or at least be married.

I really like (fill in name of a guy you have a great connection with but whom you'd be nervous to introduce to Mom or Dad), but I *shouldn't* date him.

I *should* have things figured out by now. This is not how I imagined my life to be at (fill in your age). How did everyone else pull all the pieces together except me?

I *should've* married (fill in name of someone you've dated in the past). Maybe that was my only shot at love.

Do any of these statements sound familiar?

I hate the word *should*. You would think it's a benign or neutral word, one that implies a suggestion you can take or leave, but it's more powerful than that. (*Should* wants you to believe that it's neutral—trust me.)

Perhaps it's because I'm a writer and sensitive to words, but *should* gets the tiny hairs on my arms to stand up. Exceptions are specific circumstances like, "I should feed the dog now, since he hasn't eaten since last night" or "I should use up my vacation days and go to Belize before the end of the year." In most cases, though, people inflect the word *should* with a slightly annoyed or apologetic tone.

Should keeps us from taking risks, connecting with our values, and following our hearts. *Should* has kept some of my friends from being with people who would have otherwise made them very happy. *Should* almost prevented me from dating the man who would become my husband.

Michael was standing in front of me for years practically waving flags that said, "Give this a chance! Have you ever been more comfortable with anyone?! Do you laugh this much with others? Are you not the best version of yourself with me?" But I missed the signs because I was convinced that he just wasn't my type.

I felt I should be with someone more polished and sophisticated. (Not that I felt particularly polished and sophisticated.) I imagined that my future husband would have an impressive résumé filled with academic accomplishments and brilliant accolades. My guy would be a triple threat: smart, handsome, and successful. He and I would walk into a room and be the toast of the town. I wanted to make my family proud and inspire awe (and maybe even a little jealousy) in others with the catch I'd landed.

While I was friends with Michael, I dated a man who had graduated summa cum laude from an Ivy League school and worked as a surgeon before deciding to get an MBA and launch what would become a multimillion-dollar company. This guy looked sharp in a suit and spoke three languages. Ooh—this was the one I should be with!

So why was I daydreaming about my quirky neighbor?

For most of my 20s, I lived by shoulds. I should have an office job. I should pick the nice Jewish boy to marry. I should actually make use of one of my two degrees that cost my parents a fortune. I should not complain—I was healthy and had a loving family.

When I spoke with my aunt's friend about my relationship, she remarked, "What are you waiting for?! This guy sounds perfect! *You shouldn't be so picky.*" (Um—thanks.) I responded, "Getting married is not my challenge. Staying married—happily married— is my goal. That's what I want."

The sentence came out of my mouth before my brain registered it. It was as if I was channeling a more confident version of myself who articulated her wants without an apology (as we women often do). My brief exchange with this person—whom I will probably never see again—crystallized what I wanted and shaped the next phase of my relationship and my life.

I ended a 5-year relationship with an amazing man despite the fact that he had everything I thought I was looking for, and I entered a new chapter of consciousness and confidence. During this period, I made a deliberate decision to replace the word *should* with the word *want*.

I wanted to feel deeply connected. I wanted to feel clarity in my job, my relationships, and my life. I knew I would not feel satisfied until I had that. I even changed my e-mail password to "clarity"—trying to subliminally signal my brain that feeling clear and grounded was a top priority.

As I packed up the apartment I'd shared with my boyfriend, I cried every day, thinking of the future we had been building together and the memories we'd shared. It was one of the hardest things I have ever done; yet even after many months of sobbing and missing him, I did not regret following my gut.

I don't think we ever do.

Should is a security blanket. It feels safe. But *should* was an important word for me to give up as I stepped into a new chapter of my life. Dismissing the word *should* (or at least catching myself when I use it too much) has made me more conscious of my wants and more able to pursue goals, and relationships, that bring me great fulfillment.

"Can't" Isn't Much Better Than "Should"

So we've established that I'm not a fan of *should*, but I haven't yet told you how I feel about *can't*.

Can't doesn't impress me. *Can't* is a lazy and passive way of saying "I won't." Again, there are exceptions—like "I can't lick my elbow" (did you just try?) or "I can't speak Cantonese." But for the purposes of this book, I'm referring to the *can't* that we all say when we are not open to possibility or when we are trying something outside our comfort zone.

I've had a number of clients tell me that they *can't* join a dating site and they *can't* make time to meet new people. I ask them how they expect to be in a relationship if they don't even have time to go out during the week. When I ask them why they *can't* join an online dating service, I hear answers like these:

I *can't* go online to date because I *can't* make a connection behind a computer screen.

I *can't* go on any more blind dates.

I *can't* believe you think I would go out with the losers who are dating online!

Or when I've asked a client why she won't date someone she is obviously interested in, I've heard things like "I *can't*—my parents would freak!" or "I *can't* date someone like him."

I was once guilty of the *can'ts* myself. A few years ago, I was talking with my good friend Janna about how much I loved spending time with Michael. Janna asked the obvious question: "If you love being with him so much, why aren't you dating him?" I quickly responded, "I *can't* be with someone like him—he's not my type!"

Even though I didn't admit it at the time, I realized how silly I sounded as the words came out. I thought about those words all night. Actually, I thought about Michael all night . . .

We also use *can't* when we stay in relationships that we feel we *should* be in but that we secretly know are not working. I took a long time to end the relationship with my accomplished boyfriend because I felt I couldn't let him or my family down. "I can't leave . . ." is what I told my therapist. My reasons were based in part on my deep affection for this guy, in part on guilt. My can't reasons were fear based, as *can't* rarely comes from an empowering place.

During this period, I remember wondering if I was happy. (Here's a hint: If you're trying to figure out if you're happy, you probably aren't.) I felt completely overwhelmed by the idea of making a decision about my relationship. I was a passive participant in the situation instead of owning my part in the decision and the direction I wanted my life to take.

If I had been truly honest in those moments, I would have admitted, "I *won't* leave this because I'm scared I'll regret it and scared I'll let everyone down. I want to feel something I do not feel with this person."

When you shift your language—from *should* to *want* and from *can't* to *won't*—you will hear your disclaimers and excuses and will be able to start taking ownership of your choices.

This is when change happens.

Meet Your Gremlin

At various points in the day, your left brain produces some mind chatter that influences your attitude and helps you make decisions. Research on brain activity shows that the left hemisphere is most responsible for analytical thinking and logical reasoning. The right brain is more imaginative and focuses on the big picture over the details. The left-brain inner dialogue can either act as your cheerleader ("You're going to ace the job interview—you deserve this position!") or play the role of your gremlin ("You're a fraud. Who do you think you are, applying for this job?").

The gremlin's role is to sabotage your dreams, goals, and desires. Even the most optimistic person gets visited by her gremlin occasionally. Not surprisingly, your gremlin's best buds are *should* and *can't*.

Have you ever been close to something that you worked hard to get, and then, just before it started, you were greeted by a nasty inner voice telling you that you were going to fail? That's the gremlin. It most often wakes up when you are close to a want, perhaps because the stakes are so high. I remember the day before I started to host a show—a dream job for me. I thought about how horrible I'd look in the wardrobe, how stupid I'd sound on camera, and how I wasn't cut out for the job. I had worked for years to get to that point in my career, including going to school for broadcast journalism, but just before I started filming, I made myself sick with worry and almost had to cancel the shoot.

My client Rebecca described her gremlin's voice as that of a 90-year-old smoker who can hardly breathe. I asked Rebecca if she felt suffocated by this voice. "I can't tell. I've known her for so long, she's really familiar," Rebecca mused, adding, "but she's really a pain in the ass." As we spoke, Rebecca realized that her 90-year-old gremlin practically woke her up each morning, telling her there wouldn't be enough hours in the day to reach her goals. And my client wondered why she felt overwhelmed every day!

We are all entitled to insecurities and self-doubt; however, when this voice prevents you from engaging in life in a vibrant way, it's time to tackle your gremlin. This negative voice will try to convince you that it has your best interests in mind—but it never does.

I have a rule in this book: When you hear your gremlin's voice saying that you suck and that you *shouldn't* try something new or that you *can't* stop doing something you don't enjoy or that you *should* be doing something else, take note. Don't be fooled into thinking your gremlin is serving you. There is a difference between thoughtful introspection and unnecessary criticism. The way to distinguish between the two of them is to weigh what you are learning from each.

If your inner voice is putting you down, passing superficial judgment on someone else, or offering unhelpful insights, it's probably negatively affecting your outlook. Ask your gremlin to step aside. The most effective way to tackle a gremlin is to have a conversation with it and put it in its place!

Here's an example of a script to tackle a dating gremlin.

- *Gremlin:* Why would this guy like you? He has a million choices, so don't count on him. You're going to get hurt.

    You: Shut up. Plenty of people love hanging out with me, and I'm sure he wouldn't have asked me out if he weren't into me.

- *Gremlin:* This guy seems too nervous. Turnoff!

    You: Maybe he's nervous because he likes me. Besides, I'm not perfect either. If I don't give him a chance, I may be missing a great guy.

Easy, right? You will undoubtedly feel a little odd the first time you tackle a gremlin (especially if you converse with it out loud, which I would not recommend doing *on* a date). But by acknowledging your inner saboteur, you will realize that you do not need to put up with negativity and unhealthy perspectives.

Sometimes, your gremlin disguises itself and pretends it's planting these thoughts in your head because it cares. Not surprisingly, your gremlin's voice may be familiar to you—it might sound like your mother, your older brother, or your best friend.

- *Gremlin:* This guy lives in another city! That's going to be hard for you. You can't date him.

  You: I know it's not convenient, but I like him more than I've liked a guy in a long time. It's worth the risk.

- *Gremlin:* You deserve to be with someone who has never been married.

  You: Maybe his past experience is just what I need because he has learned from it. I deserve to be with someone who makes me happy and treats me well, and this person does.

Remember: If your gremlin is saying horrible things to you that you would never say to a friend or loved one, or is challenging you so much that you feel drained, the gremlin is not welcome!

A few years ago, one of my clients sketched her gremlin for me. It looked like an evil version of the Monster.com mascot. She said, "Every time I want to take a risk, he shakes his head in disapproval and tells me to go back to reality."

Another client explained that she has multiple gremlins that hide out in the woods. These guys won't show their faces, but they are always in a state of disapproval. She described them as cowardly.

My gremlin is a boring, messy, and disgusting blob. I don't even know if it has eyes, but I know it's lazy, insecure, and heavy—not a character that I can learn from or would ever want to hang out with.

Throughout this book, I will relate the true stories of amazing women I know, both clients and friends, who fell in love with men who were not their types. These women initially resisted and doubted their unconventional romantic choices, but those feelings faded once they realized what they found with their nontype and acknowledged how special that connection was.

The women you will meet in *He's Just Not Your Type* are dynamic, attractive, and thoughtful. In most cases, these women dated great guys in the past, not losers—but those good guys were not good partners *for them*.

These women's gremlins came out to play and their *should* and *can't* voices crept up when they initially spent time with their non-types, but in the end their *want* voices overruled the others.

I have the same wish for you.

Exercises

1. Recall a time when you gave up an opportunity because you did not think you should do it even though you wanted to. Whose voice prevented you from following your heart? What have you learned from this experience?

2. What are some of your most common *shoulds*? Create two columns on a sheet of paper. In one column, write some of the *shoulds* that are familiar, and in the other column, replace them with what you want.

Should	Want

3. What does *your* gremlin's voice sound like? If it had a face and body, what would he, she, or it look like? Sketch or find a visual depiction of your gremlin.

2

It's All about Perspective. What's Yours?

I once knew a woman whose dinner date excused himself to go to the restroom before their main courses arrived. After 20 minutes, he had not returned, and the woman asked the waiter to check on him. She was worried that her date was stuck in his bathroom stall or had become ill. The waiter reported back to her a few minutes later: "Nobody's in there." He held back laughter and said, "It looks like he may have crawled out the window, since otherwise you would've seen him leave. Do you still want your chicken?"

Funny story or depressing tale? Probably a little of both.

She laughed as she recounted the play-by-play to me. I could tell she had gotten a lot of mileage out of the anecdote and had perfected her punch line: "Miss, it looks like your date crawled out the window. Do you still want your chicken?"

While this woman was able to find humor in a bad date, many other women cite stories like this as justification to give up on dating.

Perspective is everything.

How do you view dating? Which of the following statements most accurately reflect your attitude?

Dating is funny.

I'm learning a lot.

Where I am is exactly where I need to be.

I have faith: I know in my heart it will all work out.

Dating sucks.

I'm tired of dating.

I'm losing patience.

I'm losing faith: No good guys are left.

The reality is that all of these dating perspectives can be true for you depending on the day (or the hour!).

When I was teaching a dating class in New York City, I wrote each of these perspectives on separate pieces of paper and posted the sheets around the room. Then I asked the workshop participants to walk to the sign that most resonated with them. The majority of the women gravitated to the signs that captured how tiring or difficult dating can be.

I asked one participant to justify why she chose the "I'm tired of dating" sheet.

"Dating is an exhausting exercise," she responded. "I wish I could close my eyes and be done with it." Her arms were folded and her energy was low. She was not making eye contact with anyone or anything but the floor. The other students were nodding in agreement, suggesting that they, too, were exhausted with the whole experience.

Then I asked these women to stand in front of a more

optimistic sign and defend its perspective. One woman found herself under the sign "I have faith: I know in my heart it will all work out." She looked irritated. She said, "I can't justify this sign. I don't believe it and don't want to say it just to play this game."

"Why are you here if you don't believe dating will work out for you?" I challenged her. "Why are you wasting your time in this class or spending time dating at all? Shouldn't you just give up?"

She thought about it for a minute and said, "Good point. It's just hard . . ." She started to tear up, then added, "Somewhere inside, I suppose, I believe he's out there—but I'm losing patience."

"Why do you think he's out there?" I prodded. "You're not allowed to say that you don't know. Give me one reason to justify that you know he's out there." (At this point, I'm sure she was annoyed, but I could tell the exercise was helping her.)

She thought for a couple of minutes and responded with confidence. "I know so many friends who felt like I feel, and it worked out for them. And I know, intellectually, there are millions of singles out there also looking. I'm a really good catch," she added, "so a good guy's going to have to realize that at some point!"

By now, this woman's body language had completely changed. She was a little surprised by her sassy answer. She was smiling and looked much more confident as she made eye contact with many of us in the room.

I asked her which perspective felt better to embrace—the one that focused on being tired of dating, or the one that reinforced the fact that dating would work out. She admitted that speaking from the perspective of "I have faith" clearly made her feel more inspired and empowered.

On any given day, you choose how you react to various situations, and you choose your perspective. Once you settle on a perspective, you collect evidence to support your outlook. If you think you've missed the boat, you will prove that theory by noticing all the unavailable men around you.

You may think that the way you see the world—or, more specifically, your dating life—is beyond your control and that you are being phony if you embrace a new outlook. But I believe that you can teach yourself to reframe a situation and find the lesson, the blessing, or at least the humor in dates or relationships that don't work out.

For the woman whose date crawled through a bathroom window, dating is funny.

She could have given up on men after the experience. (Imagine paying the tab after that!) Instead, she dusted herself off and added the experience to her collection of dating disaster stories. She recognized that this man was so cowardly that he was not worth crying over or being angry about. His actions said more about *him* than they did about *her*, and she knew that. Her perspective allows her to feel confident about being single.

What's Your Dating Mantra?

To shake up your dating life and find success, you need to understand your belief system about yourself and dating—and then challenge it. I have a feeling many of you have adopted your gremlin's dating slogans, statements like "Good guys are hard to find" or "Guys never like me as more than a friend."

You know those women who seem to be less interesting or less cute than you but have no problem attracting men? Do you ever wonder what their secret is? Well, for starters, their inner voices are telling them they are rock stars. What they believe about themselves is what they attract. Sounds a lot like the law of attraction, doesn't it?

For those of you who aren't already familiar with the law of attraction, which was made popular by the best-selling book *The Secret*, it refers to the belief that your thoughts have the power to become your reality. In other words, you will manifest in your life whatever you believe you deserve.

Proponents of the theory state that people must practice four things to successfully embrace the law of attraction.

1. Get clear on what you want. Be specific.
2. Ask the universe (or God, or Buddha, or whatever higher entity you ascribe to) for it.
3. Feel and behave as if the object of your desire is on its way to you.
4. Be open to receive it and let go of your attachment to the outcome.

Don't buy it? Let me appeal to your rational side:

Most of us would agree that you drive better when you are fully awake, because your motor skills and reflexes are sharp. I'm guessing that you will also agree that you do better in a job interview when you feel prepared and confident.

Scientists have studied the placebo effect, in which patients who have unknowingly ingested sugar pills in place of real medicine report feeling better. It is believed that this therapeutic effect may be the result of a physiological response initiated by the brain, which alerts the body to feel well. In other words, in these cases, the brain exerts at least some control over the physical symptoms of illness.

In a similar vein, many elite athletes use visualization techniques to achieve success. Before a race or a game, these athletes work with trainers or psychologists to visualize positive

Simple Truth: The Man You Are Looking For Is Also Looking for You

Men write me every day to say they're looking for love. So many men have told me that they feel intimidated and vulnerable in dating, or that they dream of a day when they can share their lives with a significant other. Good men are everywhere. You will find them when you start believing that to be true. Some may just come in a different package than you may have imagined.

performance. The athletes mentally review and rehearse their movements, picture the inner workings of their muscles and bones, and envision harnessing their strength to outperform the competition. Positive visualization has proven to be an effective strategy in sports.

Whether you call it the law of attraction or the placebo effect or visualization, there is a correlation between focusing on positive thoughts and performing well. And this principle applies to dating. When you are prepared and believe something is going to work, you exude confidence and energy. If you are constantly telling yourself that guys never like you or that no good ones are left, you're not exactly making yourself an appealing candidate. After all, which person would you approach at a party—a guy who seems insecure and stuck in his own head, or one who is radiating natural confidence and having fun?

How you feel inevitably affects how you perform and the impression you make on others.

Meet Mr. Perfect

Imagine for a moment that you find the "perfect" man (PM). He is attractive, has a great job, comes from a good family, and graduated from a top school. He's charming and intelligent and impresses people wherever he goes. He's witty, sociable, and extremely driven. This guy is in your age range and is exactly what you always pictured your husband to be.

If I told you that you could be finished with dating and sign up for a life with this person, would you say yes? After all, many women I've interviewed claim that these are the exact criteria they look for in long-term mate.

What more could a woman want?

Before you decide to marry this made-to-order man, let's get to know him a little more. . . .

It is true that PM is attractive. And he knows it—he spends more time in front of the mirror than you do.

It is true that PM has a great job and makes a handsome salary. You will soon find out that he is so successful because he is a workaholic. He works 12 to 14 hours a day and always brings work home—even on weekends. He misses a lot of important family events—or even simple ones, like dinner with you—because he's made work his top priority.

Yes, PM's family is well regarded and successful—but his mom is protective of her precious son and tries to undermine your relationship. She competes with any woman in his life. You soon understand what it means to have a "monster-in-law."

Mr. Perfect has been told about his merits all his life. He is slightly ambivalent about settling down with you because he knows how many options he has. And while it's true that he is charming and makes each individual feel like the most important person in the room, you eventually realize that this charm is a manufactured quality. Behind closed doors, when you're alone with PM, you see how self-involved and self-centered he is. He rarely thinks of you or your best interests when making decisions or plans.

This guy may decide to marry you because he cares about you and it is the appropriate time in his life to marry. In other words, he feels he *should*.

Does this man still look like the person you want to share your life with? Has your perspective changed now that you can see him through a different lens?

Of course, there are eligible and attractive men who have amazing values and are kinder and more sensitive than the man in this example. Being a "great catch" and a truly good person and partner are not mutually exclusive by any means.

The issue, though, is that when we find a man who initially adds up the way Mr. Perfect does, we may ignore the red flags that signal that he is more self-centered or selfish than we would like or that his family may be problematic later on.

Our judgment is clouded when we meet a great catch, and who could blame us? People everywhere around us reinforce how lucky we are to land such a man. Friends are jealous; parents may suggest a list of wedding venues after meeting this guy for the first time. He captures the hearts of everyone, as he did when he first met you.

When a man doesn't look or play the part of PM, it's a lot harder to convey to your friends or family how perfect he is for you. They may encourage you to keep looking around, because "You could do better."

Perhaps a guy like PM would never appeal to you in the first place because you are not generally attracted to someone that polished. Your vision of Mr. Perfect may be an artistic or bohemian guy whom you associate with great style and tremendous creativity.

My friend Susan claims that any man who lives above 14th Street in Manhattan—which is considered by some to be the less-unique "uptown" part of the city—is not cool or interesting. She dismisses guys who seem conservative or buttoned up. If she sees a guy uptown in "boring shoes," she will immediately write him off. Conversely, Susan assumes that guys she meets downtown who dress in a certain way or who hang out at particular places are her best prospects. The funny thing is, Susan cannot point to one healthy or fulfilling relationship she has had with any of the men from below 14th Street. The men whom she was instantly drawn to because they seemed deep and passionate have proven to be self-involved and flaky. These guys had cool shoes, yes, but they had little regard for Susan's feelings.

A couple of years ago. I tried to set up Susan with John, an "uptown" guy from 82nd Street. "He doesn't even live near an express stop on the subway!" she moaned. John wears nondescript shoes and works as a consultant. I told Susan that he was hilarious and thoughtful and that they would appreciate each other's sense of humor. She responded, "Consultants are boring guys who probably went to business school and didn't know what to do after they graduated, so they picked the path of least resistance."

From my perspective, consultants are often extremely creative. They find and implement outside-the-box solutions that make businesses run more efficiently. Many of my consultant friends have traveled the world, and some speak multiple languages. John lives on 82nd Street because he is a nature lover and wants to be near Central Park. He likes to run on weekends. He enjoys traveling and live comedy. But Susan was not interested. She had constructed a negative story in her mind about a person

Choose Abundance, Not Scarcity

Life is more fulfilling when you feel an abundance of possibilities rather than a scarcity of opportunities. The proverbial glass that is half full—rather than half empty—makes a situation more enjoyable.

Many people place their dates under a microscope, closely scrutinizing every quality or idiosyncrasy and determining why those characteristics will not fit in with their lives. Some women "test" men they date to see if they are worthy.

In any healthy relationship, you will find faults with your partner. Part of the healthy perspective shift that occurs when you're dating outside the box is choosing to see your mate through an abundant lens instead of a scarce one. When you make this shift in perspective, you will notice that the amazing qualities he possesses outweigh the ones he lacks.

On your next date, choose to look at what your date has rather than focus on what he is missing. Ultimately, you may decide that he is not a match, but at least you will not rule him out before discovering his strengths.

After all, wouldn't you want to be given the same chance?

she had never met. She put John in the "boring" box, and he didn't have a shot.

John laughed when I told him about Susan's 14th Street rule and thanked me for not making the introduction. He felt Susan sounded too "high maintenance." John is now married to a dynamic woman, and Susan is still dating guys who are her *type*. "Yeah—they've flaked!" she said recently about the guys she usually dates, "but they keep things interesting, and I can't help who I'm attracted to."

A moment later, she complained that there were no good guys left.

Best Investment: Mutual Fun, Not Mutual Funds

A single 30-something woman once told me that she was only interested in Wall Street types and businessmen. She outlined the appropriate jobs for her future husband: investment banker, hedge fund manager, real estate developer. She didn't realize I was not a professional matchmaker, and she hoped I'd find her a *perfect* man.

As I write this, America is experiencing one of its darkest economic chapters since the Great Depression. An investment banker recently joked with me that he used to rely on his job title to impress women. Now he needs a new game (and a new job). He's been laid off.

Don't get me wrong, I'm a big fan of financial security. It would be silly and naive not to place any importance on this aspect of our lives when choosing a life partner—especially since money problems are one of the primary causes of divorce.

The issue I have with placing so much value on qualities such as good looks and a great job is that they are fleeting. These two factors are probably the worst long-term investments when choosing a life partner. There are no guarantees that a marriage founded on good looks and great careers will stand the test of time.

Expand Your Scope

Early in 2009, months after the beginning of the stock market crash, the *New York Times* ran an article on members of a support group and blog called DABA (Dating a Banker Anonymous). Its members were New York City women who were dating or were married to bankers and now found themselves in danger of losing the ritzy life they thought they had signed up for. The blog, which grew rapidly, encouraged women to share their stories and join the community "if your monthly Bergdorf's allowance has been halved and bottle service has all but disappeared from your life."

One member lamented in her post, "The question undoubtedly on every DABIT's mind since she moved to NYC has been 'Where has the party gone?' We were promised the good life. (You've got some explaining to do, Candace Bushnell!)"

If you wake up with nothing in common with your husband—because you never really did have anything in common with him besides good looks and enjoying the good life—perhaps that's a result of placing too much emphasis on short-term qualities.

It's more important to choose a mate based on his financial smarts and drive rather than the balance in his checking account. The way a man relates to and respects his money is more telling about his long-term behavior than how much money he's making when you meet him.

My husband is a hard worker and has no debt on a teacher's salary because he is responsible and thoughtful about his spending. I love that about him. Meanwhile, one of my exes who made plenty of money lived an extravagant lifestyle beyond his means, forcing him to consolidate numerous credit cards to maintain the life he believes he deserves.

Before walking down the aisle, each prospective bride must explore whether or not the man she wants to marry will be fiscally responsible in tough times. However, we generally use the wrong information to assess the financial reality of a potential mate. It is not that he *has* money but *how he is* with money that should be examined before you enter a legal partnership. Does your guy have debt? If so, how much? How does he plan to pay it back? Is your man generous or stingy? Does he buy expensive items for himself but spend frugally on you or others? The answers to these questions—this perspective—will tell you far more about your financial future together than his job title does.

The way we measure a "great catch" is far too short sighted, but society reinforces this stereotype all around us. In the next chapter, I will share some checklists you can use to more accurately determine whether or not someone is a good catch for *you*.

There's a Fine Line between Endearing and Annoying

My friend Isla once complained to her daughter and her boyfriend that she was fat. Her daughter disagreed: "You're not fat, Mom, you're obese!" Isla's boyfriend disagreed and said, "You're not fat, Isla, you're amazingly voluptuous!"

Perspective is important when it comes to selecting a mate. What you may see as arrogance in a guy may be viewed by another woman as sexy. What one person finds annoying, another may find endearing.

Consider a couple I knew years ago. The husband checked in with his wife for everything: what to wear, what to order, how to talk to his boss, which route to take home . . . It seemed that he called his wife with questions every 5 minutes. I'm someone who needs more space; I couldn't imagine dating someone like him. I even found myself mouthing "What?!" every time I heard his wife pick up the phone and happily exclaim, "It's Jonathan again!" But this woman found it sweet that her mate could barely last an hour without her. She gushed about how romantic and thoughtful it was that he was in touch all day.

I considered this man to be overbearing, but his wife saw his actions as caring. We both were right. In some cases, it's a matter of individual taste and how each person views the same quality— and sometimes it's simply based on chemistry.

Every character trait is a double-edged sword. You may love someone's spontaneity but find it frustrating that he won't commit to attending events until the last minute. Or you may love a guy's gentle nature but get frustrated when he won't assert himself.

Depending on your perspective, here are just a few ways you might perceive the same quality in a person:

Workaholic or driven
Annoying or playful
Slow or relaxed
Old or experienced
Overbearing or caring
Neurotic or sensitive
Odd or unique

A *word of warning*: Although I believe there are two sides to every character trait, sometimes the glass really *is* half empty. If a man is inconsiderate, disrespectful, abusive, or unkind, I do not believe that you should consider the other side. Walk away.

Interestingly, when you date and get to know your nontype, your initial assessment of his compatibility with you often changes. For instance, if your NT is a single father—something that may initially worry you—you may later find yourself citing his family values as one of his best qualities. What initially concerns you about your NT may be the very thing that you appreciate about him and your relationship later.

My friend Madeline had this experience with her NT, Tom, who is 16 years older than she is. Madeline originally saw Tom's age as an obstacle. Other people warned her about how problematic it could be in their future. Madeline now sees Tom's age from a new vantage point: "Tom introduces me to things I never would be exposed to *because* he's older. He's seen the world, and I learn a lot from him. That's so important to me. Learning is one of my greatest joys. I'm never bored with Tom, and I know I never will be. I think this is how I knew he was the one I wanted to share my life with."

When I first started dating Michael, some people questioned my choice. They were used to me dating "successful" men, and they thought I deserved the lifestyle they could provide.

When I fell for Michael, for the first time in my life I challenged my own definition of success. I realized that a successful man was one who nurtured and supported the well-being of our home and contributed to our emotional savings account. He would regularly deposit love, respect, and open communication. He would make his marriage and his family a priority.

My husband teaches kids and gives back to his community. He is wonderfully present for me emotionally and contributes equally to our home. He has tremendous integrity and puts family first.

I thought I wanted to be with the man who made six figures, but it turns out I'm happiest with the man who is home by six.

Widen Your Scope

I have interviewed a number of singles who think they have bad luck in dating. The common thread among them is that they are repeating a dating pattern that isn't working (which reinforces negative messages about how difficult dating is) and they view their dating life and the men they meet through a narrow, negative lens. If you stay myopic and believe that love is a matter of black and white, you will sabotage your chances for happiness. In fact, many people who believe they are unlucky in love share the same problem: They are resistant to thinking outside the box or confronting their own patterns.

To find lasting love, you must embrace a perspective that is vibrant and panoramic. Stay open to all the possibilities and people along the way. Believe that even if it takes time and patience to meet your match, you will. And know that every experience deepens your learning (even when your date crawls out a bathroom window).

Exercises

You're 90 years old and looking back at your life. What advice would you give yourself now about dating? What kind of a man have you ended up with, and what has made your marriage work?

Dating Dare #1: New Perspective

Pick a positive dating perspective from the list on page 16 and justify why it's true here:

_____

_____

_____

Think of the NTs you know. Is there another—more positive—perspective you can choose when you consider some of the traits they have that are not *ideal*?

Dating Dare #2: New Dating Mantra

What love label do you wear? Pick a new love label that captures why any man you date is lucky to be with you and write it here:

_____

Commit to saying this mantra every morning when you wake up and every night before you go to bed.

I have a client whose mantra is: *I am a beautiful and shiny magnet who attracts good guys.* She swears that every time she says that to herself while walking down the street she gets more attention. She recently told me that a guy ran after her on a busy street in midtown Manhattan to pass along his business card. She wasn't interested in him (and not because he wasn't her type!), but she felt like she had a newly acquired superpower.

Dating Dare #3: Step into Character

Think of a woman whose social approach and confidence you admire. She could be a celebrity, a character on TV or in a book, a friend, or a woman you met once but who made a positive impression. How would this woman walk into a room? Imagine her body language. How would she approach strangers? Why would strangers be attracted to her?

For a month, try channeling this woman when you enter social situations. See if anything shifts in how you feel and whom you attract.

3

The New Checklists for Love

Education consists mainly in what we have unlearned.

—Mark Twain

When I was 16, my "type" was a guy who drove a motorcycle, had two earrings, and grunted when I asked him questions. I don't remember ever having a deep conversation with this guy, Ryan, but I remember how good he looked in a white T-shirt and tight acid-wash jeans. (Hey, it was the '80s.)

At age 20, I dated a guy in my college dorm who was whiter than Wonder Bread and who found my Jewishness exotic. He was a good kisser, and I liked that he found it endearing when I argued that bagels were a food group. But really, I had nothing in common with him, and I knew it.

When you're young and new to dating, a guy's cool factor or the way he looks in jeans may rank higher than your emotional or spiritual connection or his ability to bring out your great qualities. At this point in your life, your criteria for a mate aren't usually based on what kind of a father, provider, and lifelong partner he would be. In many ways, our teen years and early 20s are about exploration—learning who we are and making mistakes from which we ultimately grow. And yet I meet so many women who still hang on to the type of guy they were attracted to eons ago. Most of these women have friends who are different from the ones they chose as teenagers, and many of them have embarked on career paths that diverge from what they chose to study in school. In other words, their choices and their lifestyles have evolved—but their taste in men has not.

If you have not edited your type in the past few years, or if you haven't learned what you want in a future partner based on what past partners have lacked, it's no wonder that you're repeating an unsuccessful dating pattern.

So many of us get in a rut in love and our lives. We do things the way we have always done them. We don't question our routines because it is comfortable. We do what we know. We are creatures of habit, after all.

When we live in this passive way, it is like pressing a snooze button on our lives. We are almost awake—but not quite. (Isn't it interesting that sleep researchers say that pressing snooze repeatedly in the morning actually makes for a less productive day?) And when we do not live consciously, we make choices that may not serve our best interests.

Similarly, choosing to date the same kind of man (the one you call your type) even when you realize past relationships haven't worked is not the best strategy. Yet I often hear women say things like "I always date jerks who break my heart" or "I date guys I'm not so attracted to" as if they have no control over this reality.

You may hear me repeat this a few hundred more times: I do not believe in bad luck in dating, just bad choices.

Wake Up!

You are the constant in every relationship. Stop being complacent, stop being satisfied with what you know, and stop being a bystander. For change to happen, you must create it.

We've all heard the famous line from the poem "In Memoriam" by Alfred, Lord Tennyson: " 'Tis better to have loved and lost than never to have loved at all." I would edit this advice to read: It's better to have loved and *learned* than never to have loved at all.

The first step in changing an unsuccessful dating pattern is to identify your pattern. Ask yourself the following questions:

1. If your dating life were a book, what would it be titled? How would it begin and end? Who would be the pursuer and who the object of pursuit?
2. Most of us have a dating pattern. What is yours?
3. What kind of man do you generally date? What are the qualities you look for in a mate? Write them down.

OkCupid.com, one of world's largest free online dating sites, helped me conduct some research for this book. In one poll, they sent e-mails to hundreds of female subscribers asking the women to describe their types. Here's a sampling of their answers.

"Extroverted, confident, cocky."

"I always thought I had a type, but it's been varied."

"Someone who's charming and charismatic, who wants to be the center of attention."

"The Funny Bouncer: big, tall, protective, with a sense of humor."

"Nerdy, intellectual, glasses, longish hair."

"About 6 foot, dark hair, dark eyes; glasses are a *must*."

"I usually go for burly men with lots of body hair and love
   handles. And I prefer strong men who can pick me up
   and throw me around."

"I'm more physically attracted to the indie, alternative type
   of guys. I just love their style, and they are usually nice."

"Skinny, stoner looking, untucked shirt, stylish (not trendy
   though). I prefer longer hair."

Most of these responses speak to the look or personal style of a
man. Few reference the way these men make the women feel or
detail the qualities likely to ensure long-term relationship success.
The women polled were clearly typecasting—attaching specific
characteristics to a guy with a certain look or sensibility.

Talking about Evolution (Your Evolution)

I was talking to a friend about the idea of dating the nontype. She
said, "Why are you encouraging women to pursue men who don't
look like their ideal mate? Why should they settle for less than the
best or less than what they dream about?"

Let me be clear: I don't want you to settle. In fact, I ask you to
do the opposite: I challenge you to challenge yourself. Taking the
easy route—living your life on autopilot—and simply going for
what you've gone for in the past, what looks best on paper, or what
others tell you is right for you . . . well, *that's* settling. How many
times have I heard of a "perfect" couple who have broken up? I
think of *settling* in a different way, I suppose.

Many of us get attached to a picture of an ideal mate and make choices based on a fantasy rather than on what we really want in life. It takes more work to challenge our beliefs about what will make us happy.

Set standards. High standards. I don't think you should settle when you settle down. Instead, consider that the criteria—the checklists—you currently use may not lead to long-term fulfillment in a relationship. For this reason, it is time to reevaluate your love lists.

Tall, Dark, Handsome

We are bombarded by messages that tell us what kind of man will make us happy—even though we are individuals with unique sets of values and preferences. Why are we comparing our cars, our clothes, and our men to those of people we hardly know or friends whose lives may be entirely different from what we observe from the outside? It is presumptuous, really, to assume those people—the ones whose lives we envy—are happy. Some are, but I am willing to bet there are women with "perfect" homes or husbands who would trade places with the woman who found true love with a partner who made her feel adored, expressed, and fulfilled.

My friend Jenny married a man who seemed like the ideal mate. He doted on her, pitched in with housework, and made us all laugh. He was kind and considerate. He was an amazing musician. Everybody liked him, and many of us wanted to find someone just like him. Less than a year into Jenny's marriage, we were surprised to learn that her husband was moving out. I remember thinking that if *they* didn't have a shot, there was no way I could stay in a marriage. (Did I mention that my love label when I was single was "commitment-phobe"?)

I learned later that the picture I had painted of my friend and her husband's relationship was very different from reality. Jenny and her husband had hardly touched each other since the first year that they dated. She had believed things would change once they made the union official, but that didn't happen. She admits that she often felt lonely in her marriage. She did not follow her gut feeling that it wasn't *right* to marry someone with whom there was little physical intimacy.

Another woman I know, Maki, thought that intellectual men were her ultimate type. Maki listed "avid reader" and "academic achievement" as the most essential qualities for a mate. She wanted to be mentally stimulated and challenged. Maki admits now that she forgot to list other essential criteria, like kindness and emotional stability, on her checklist.

Maki married a guy who challenged her, but not in a healthy or constructive way. He was negative and insecure and lacked emotional intelligence. He felt the world was out to get him. He had a lot of anger that he took out on Maki, her friends, his family, and even the waitstaff at restaurants. Although Maki saw his anger and anxiety before they got married, she thought he would be more healthy and stable in the right relationship.

Both Jenny and Maki married what they perceived to be their types. Each of these men represented what Jenny and Maki believed they were looking for; however, both women focused on the man's *potential*, not the reality, and they ignored their instincts that the relationships felt wrong. Over time, both women realized that they were not fulfilled in their marriages. Their husbands possessed what Jenny and Maki initially thought were the most important qualities, but those qualities were not enough to sustain a happy relationship.

What if this woman who seems to have it all—from an outsider's perspective—is you?

I've talked to too many women who woke up one day and realized that they were in an unfulfilling marriage because they hadn't been honest with themselves about what they needed to be happy. "I thought I was doing the right thing when I got married the first time," one such woman admitted. "He treated me like a princess, and he had a great job. I ignored the fact that he was socially awkward and a little codependent on me since I admired a lot about him. I made excuses to myself to justify why I was marrying him. I should have known by the way I felt on my wedding day—or the day he proposed to me—that this wasn't the guy for me. I had a knot in my stomach. And moments before walking down the aisle, I was asked by a friend, 'Are you sure you want to marry him?' That's never a good sign! I insisted that this was the guy for me until I woke up one day in my marriage and realized I did not want to grow old with this man. I did not see him as the father of my kids. It was an overwhelming feeling in the core of my being, and I listened to it for the first time."

If you speak to a woman who has broken off an engagement (by now, most of us know at least one), you will hear the same theme: She felt she *should* be with a man like the one she was planning to marry, and she didn't want to let anyone down by not marrying him.

My friend Kelly realized she did not want to go through with her wedding to Brent the very night he was celebrating his bachelor party. She had been with Brent for 7 years and had always thought she would marry him and have a great life. "Brent was perfect on paper," Kelly said. "He was super-educated, came from a great and wealthy family, had a huge heart and amazing social graces. He could charm anyone (and it was genuine). He worshipped me. He was my best friend. We didn't fight. We traveled around the world. People would tell me we had a dream relationship. My mom still talks about him, and we ended our relationship years ago."

This man was everything Kelly thought she wanted in a partner, and she loved him—so why did she call off her wedding? Kelly said she never completely understood her decision. In the weeks before the wedding, she felt uncomfortable in her own skin. "I didn't recognize myself," she said. "I experienced major chest pains, and I couldn't eat. I knew I didn't have the feeling a bride should have before she gets married. I couldn't articulate it, but my body forced me to admit that I didn't want to marry Brent before my mind understood what was happening. I was guided by this overwhelming physical feeling that would not let me move forward."

In the end, it didn't matter that Kelly couldn't understand her confusion. She was not acting like herself and was wasting away from anxiety. She knew she had to confront what was happening and face her fear of letting everybody down.

Kelly admitted that she was living by shoulds when she got engaged. "I thought I was really happy and knew that everyone around me was getting married . . . so Brent and I felt we should do that, too."

What advice would Kelly give to other women who stayed in relationships because they felt they should? "No matter what, you have to speak your truth, or it will find you," she said.

Today, Kelly looks back on the experience as one of great learning, despite the sadness and difficult months that followed. She knows now that she will never settle for a man who does not give her the *feeling* she wants to have. "Even if it takes me until I'm 55 years old, I won't settle for someone unless I have clarity that I really want to be with him. I could have married a perfect guy—so why would I settle now?"

The New Checklists for Love

Your list of criteria for a future mate should not resemble your lengthy grocery-shopping list or the apartment- or house-hunting checklist you hand your real estate agent. For one thing, you decrease your chances of finding a relationship if your love list is too long and specific; for another, a long checklist takes the romance and spontaneity out of truly connecting with someone you have not met yet! I once heard a guy say that he could not describe his perfect woman before he met her, just as he can't describe a beautiful painting before he has seen it. Depending on your perspective, this guy is either wonderfully romantic or terribly cheesy . . . but he has a point!

Even though I do not like the checklists many singles are currently using, I do think it is important to be mindful and aware of the qualities you would like to find in your mate. (Remember the law of attraction from Chapter 2?) I have created three kinds of checklists to guide you in this process:

1. Passions and Core Values
2. The Four Essential Ingredients
3. Must-Haves and Can't Stands

Checklist #1: Passions and Core Values

Passions

What are you passionate about? When I ask this question, some women stare blankly at me and shrug. A woman once responded, "I'm just not passionate about anything, I guess . . . as if it was a matter of fact.

My hunch is that if you have a pulse, you have a passion. Since passion makes life a whole lot more meaningful and fun, and since passion ranks as one of the sexiest qualities you can have to attract a mate, I think it's time to think about yours.

Here's a list of some of the things that I'm passionate about:

- Eating good food (especially cookies or anything that involves cheese and bread)
- Music
- Performing
- Laughing every day
- Traveling
- Learning
- Living consciously
- Helping people discover their true potential
- Taking risks
- Watching movies
- Reading
- Writing
- Being physically active (especially walking and swimming)
- Dogs
- Connecting with friends and family

(Did I mention some of us have too many things we're passionate about to be confined to a page?!)

What's on Your Passion List?

Now it's your turn to list your passions. *Hint:* If nothing comes to mind immediately, think about how you would spend your days if time and resources weren't issues. Indulge!

Using your passions as a guiding force in your dating life is a great strategy. When you focus on what resonates most with you, your life becomes richer and more fulfilling, and you're more likely to make romantic connections. (Besides, when you're living life *without* passion, you're more prone to getting a serious case of the blahs and ending up like that woman from the New York City dating seminar who couldn't even stomach the thought of dating. Don't become her!)

One of the top questions I get as a relationship expert is "Where do I meet someone?"

Part of the challenge and fun of finding love where you least expect it is going outside your comfort zone. If you keep looking in the same places, you will see the *same* people. Not a good strategy for meeting new people, is it?

Where are all the interesting men you *haven't* met? When I posed this question to one of my clients, she challenged herself to try a salsa class. She laughed, "I'll feel like a dork, but at least nobody will recognize me!" She had never gone anywhere close to the salsa scene. While my client did not meet a guy at her first dance lesson, she had a lot of fun learning new steps and meeting new people. More important, she realized that breaking up her usual Saturday-night routine opened up a whole new set of possibilities. She felt excited about dating again.

Another one of my clients, Abby, often told me her type was a conservative, cute, and clean-cut guy. When I asked her to delve deeper, she mentioned that intelligence is the sexiest characteristic a man could have. She also appreciated someone a little quirky who would understand her unique sense of style and humor. She added, "I think I even like nerds!" One weekend soon after our conversation, Abby drove from Los Angeles to a comic book convention in San Diego. She met a great guy there. Even though they went out only a few times, she realized what kind of man she could meet if she stayed open. The experience gave her renewed confidence and made the prospect of future blind dates more appealing.

Abby is now dating a guy she would never have considered had she not pushed herself outside her comfort zone. Meeting all kinds of men and trying something in a different frame of reference helped Abby find the kind of person she was really looking for.

Knowing what *you* are passionate about helps guide you to people with similar interests. If you are cerebral and a little shy, a bar is probably not the place to showcase your best self. Maybe a local museum tour, class, or book club would provide an environment in which you shine.

When I met my friend Raquel, she was 36 years old and sick of being single. The dating homework I gave her was to rediscover her passion for photography, since photography was once important in her life but she had not connected with it in many years. I asked her to stop pressuring herself to meet a man tomorrow and to focus instead on her passion today.

A few months later, Raquel produced an amazing photo exhibit. She invited close friends and family, and some of us brought others to the event. That evening, she glowed with a new-found sense of confidence and glided from person to person. She owned the room and was focused on her love of art and photography. She was in her element.

One of the new people who came, Matt, walked in, introduced himself to Raquel, and complimented her work. He didn't remember that he'd actually met her months before—this new, confident version of Raquel was so utterly different from the woman he'd previously met. When they were first introduced, Raquel had been immediately attracted to Matt and his energy (did I mention this all took place in California?), but he had been oblivious. Raquel had felt a little invisible and figured he wasn't interested.

That night at the photo show, Raquel knew she had a shot (excuse the pun) when she noticed that Matt was sticking around and clearly trying to engage her in conversation.

Matt is different from Raquel's ex-boyfriends, who tended to be a little older, and more cynical and edgy. Matt is smart but has a happy, puppy-dog-like disposition and is almost 6 years younger than Raquel. He was not her type. But they quickly began dating.

The age difference was initially an issue for Raquel, who had a hard time believing that a guy in his early 30s would want to pair up with a woman approaching 40. Usually, she thought, men preferred a younger woman (unless the woman in question had aged as gracefully as Demi or Halle).

Raquel was 38 and Matt was 33 when they married.

We will revisit Raquel and Matt later, but it is worth mentioning that the spark started with passion . . . Raquel's passion.

I am not asking you to stage an event to meet a guy (that would be a time-consuming and expensive dating strategy). The point is that when you are connected to your passions, you are more likely to make decisions and attract men who are right for you.

Core Values

As you compile your "love list," also think about your core values. When you are aligned with your values, you are your most authentic self. When you are not aligned with your values, life can feel off-balance and confusing.

If you love the outdoors and nature and you are stuck in a big metropolitan area where all you see is cement, chances are you do not feel inspired. If you value learning and you can do your job with your eyes closed, you are probably not fulfilled at work. The same sense of discomfort and discontent will manifest if you are dating a person who does not reflect or support your values.

What Are Your Core Values?
Here are some questions to help you discover what is most important to you. The likelihood is that you will find some themes that run through all of your answers.

I did this exercise with my friend Selena. She volunteered to share her answers.

1. My favorite way to spend a weekend is to:
   - *Relax with a good book or the paper.*
   - *Catch up with a good friend over brunch.*
   - *Hit a bunch of parties or a cool new restaurant with some friends.*
   - *Spend time outdoors—hiking, walking, playing sports.*
   - *Explore a new gallery or exhibit in town.*

2. If time and resources were not an issue, I would spend my life:
   Traveling.

3. Two people I admire most are:
   My grandparents. They are 99 and 98 years old and have been married 76 years. They started out as street peddlers, sewing pants and selling them off the street in China, and they ended up with a very successful tie business in Hong Kong. Their success allowed them to send their children to school in the United States and Canada, where all of the family has settled since. I admire their commitment to each other and the struggle and sacrifices they made to ensure a better future for the next generations of the family.

4. The thing that I find most annoying about some people is:

Their selfishness and lack of awareness of others around them. Entitlement probably bothers me most of all.

5. It is 10 years from now. You are being honored at a social function. What is being said about you?

   I hope that the honor would be for helping a lot of people with the combination of passion, a big heart, and a bit of innovative smarts.

6. Describe a seminal experience (a moment, a day, a particular year) when you felt really good about your life. What was happening around this time? Who were you being?

   The first thing that comes to mind is the period during the year of my separation and divorce. I felt really proud of who I was during that tough time. I saw myself as a person of integrity and genuine commitment. Yet it was also a time of rediscovering myself. I traveled a lot, and I embraced all of the unique opportunities that arose for me during that year.

7. What is your favorite part of your job?

   I am a social worker, so there are a lot of tough moments in my work, but my favorite thing is knowing that everything I do has significance in someone's life.

8. What is the best vacation you ever took and why?

   Brazil has to be my favorite. During my time there, I explored the Amazon and connected to the people, language, and culture. It was defining for me in that I learned that I really enjoy being a fish out of water. I enjoy trips that expose me to new things and are challenging.

Answer these eight questions yourself. When you look over your responses, do you notice any common threads? What are they?

Selena's responses indicate that she values embracing challenges in life to overcome adversity, making a difference in the lives of others, and continually reflecting on her own life and personal growth. Adventure, passion, and commitment are other themes in Selena's responses. She cites her grandparents' commitment to each other and the commitment she wants to be recognized for in her work. All of these values reflect what is most important to Selena and will help her determine the kind of partner she will work best with. Selena's future partner should share some of her values and appreciate and respect the values she has that he does not share.

Completing this exercise helped one of my clients recognize that her ex-boyfriends possessed few of the qualities she most valued—and that they didn't support or admire those qualities in her. "Two guys who broke my heart were very self-centered," she said. "They took advantage of my ability to give and were unapologetic about it. I can't imagine why I tried so hard to make it work, considering they didn't possess the qualities that I deem as most important."

Your values are the essence of who you are. What you value and what your partner values make up your relationship DNA. We often hear that opposites attract; however, what is generally not mentioned is that even though a happy couple of "opposites" may look mismatched, upon further investigation you'll usually find that they share important common values or at least a deep respect for one another's values.

If you feel that your passions are supported in a relationship, you're more likely to be fulfilled. Conversely, relationships will seem like a struggle when values and passions clash. If you value security and your mate values adventure, that may be the seed of some of your most frequent arguments.

I am not advocating that you date a carbon copy of yourself. Not only would that be creepy, it would also be boring. You don't have to share all of the same interests—my friend Selena loves skydiving, but she should not write off a guy who doesn't feel like jumping out of a plane! She should, however, make sure that the person she is with will not try to dissuade her from participating in the adventurous activities she loves, otherwise she is likely to feel misunderstood and resentful.

The important thing is that you are seen—and celebrated—for who you are. When looking for your match, consider not only who he is but who *you* are with him. Do you feel sexy, smart, funny, and confident with the man you're dating? Do you sense that he sees the sides of you that your best girlfriends know well? Do you feel fully expressed and your most authentic self?

When you are living a life aligned with your values and passions, you will find yourself in balance and at peace. This is an important component of your love list.

Checklist #2: The Four Essential Ingredients

Naturally, you want to find someone who reflects your values and embraces your passions. Your mate should also fulfill your needs for four essential roles: partner, friend, companion, and lover.

1. Partner

Sometimes we get so caught up in the qualities we're looking for in a person that we forget there's a big difference between dating a great person and finding a great *partner*.

A partner is someone who is aligned with your values and

appreciates the meaning of compromise. He realizes that his happiness is directly affected by your own. He will do whatever it takes to get your relationship to a place of mutual respect and understanding because he knows that the ultimate goal is for two people to be happy—not just one.

I was talking about the concept of a partner with someone I used to work with. She admitted that as much as she loved her ex, he was not the kind of partner she needs in her life. She said, "It's a shame, because he's a fine person; but when life would get difficult or when we needed to compromise, he would disappear and shut down. I now know that I need a partner who can communicate and work through issues with me or meet me halfway. That's a must. I want someone who knows the real meaning of being a partner."

A true partnership is about both people being mindful of each other's needs and working together to create a happier and healthier relationship.

You may define a suitable partner differently than I would. This is how my love list looked before I dated Michael:

In a life partner, I am looking for someone who . . .

- Supports me in my personal and professional goals.
- Has a good relationship with his family and respects mine.
- Inspires me to live with him in the moment but is thoughtful about our future.
- Contributes to the emotional and physical well-being of our home.
- I can laugh and learn with.

- I'm attracted to and who is attracted to me.
- Is a good communicator and can anticipate, and is thoughtful about, my needs.
- Makes me feel like the sexiest, sassiest, and best version of myself.

What are you looking for in a life partner? Write down at least five needs or values.

1. _____
2. _____
3. _____
4. _____
5. _____

Now think about some of the men who have broken up with you or left you heartbroken in the past. Did they fulfill your "good partner" list?

2. Friend

Friendship may be the easiest relationship to define, although, at times, it is one of the most challenging. The word *friend* is both a noun and a verb.

When you are friends with your significant other, you genuinely enjoy your downtime together. You still have a close group of friends outside of your relationship, but your mate ranks as one of your best buddies. Hanging out with him is generally fun and fulfilling. When you can check off the friend box thanks to your man, you know he will be there for you on an emotional level. You can share your vulnerabilities as much as you can celebrate your triumphs. He is not competitive with you; he wants to help you succeed. It is essential that your mate is also your good friend.

That said, many women choose to be in romantic relationships with men who would have made better friends than partners. A woman I met on vacation last year told me she'd married her best friend but admitted that bond wasn't enough to sustain her marriage. "It's a big misconception," she explained. "Of course you want to spend your life with your best friend, but you also want to have physical intimacy and attraction for each other, or you may not be fulfilled in the marriage. I certainly wasn't."

Other women I've interviewed have mentioned that their partner's competitiveness created tension in the relationship, and they rarely felt natural just hanging out with their mate as friends would.

Have you ever dated someone who didn't feel like a good friend to you? In what way(s)?

3. Companion

I have an 83-year-old friend who refers to the women he dates as his "companions." He doesn't consider his companions to be friends, since he says they are "more than that." I'm not sure if they are intimate (I don't think I want to know), but he defines *companion* as a woman he spends a lot of time with and who shares similar interests and hobbies.

I once heard that the difference between a companion and a friend is that a companion is physically there to participate in events and life moments with you, while a friend is more of an emotional presence, there to provide support through events and life moments, not necessarily to attend them with you.

One of my clients explains that her loneliness comes from the fact that she has not yet met a companion, someone she can count on as her "plus one."

When you think of a companion, who comes to mind? What qualities does that person have?

4. Lover

A number of women underestimate the importance of selecting a long-term mate who is also a good lover. I believe sexual intimacy is one of the most crucial components of a successful marriage. After all, you can find friends who fulfill many of the things you are looking for in a mate, but your life partner is distinguished by the fact that you have a sexual relationship with him and nobody else (unless you're in an open marriage, which is the subject of a different book!).

It's essential that your mate is more than just a friend or companion. For example, when I visit a museum with my husband, he practically scales the walls in boredom. It took me a couple of years to realize that instead of pressuring Michael to see the new Byzantine exhibit with me, I can ask a friend to join me who will enjoy checking out the ancient relics. But I can't really recruit a friend to join me in bed on a cold night. I'm shocked by how many women knowingly enter sexless marriages, believing, perhaps, that their partner will become a lover when the commitment is legally sanctioned.

When you are selecting a mate for the long term, you want to be able to place a checkmark on your love list next to physical intimacy and compatability.

Have you ever been close to marriage with a person whom you would not consider to be your lover? What did you learn from that experience?

Tally Your Ingredients

I'm sure in a past relationship you have been able to check off one or two of these four categories. In one of my past long-term relationships, I could proudly check off "friend" and "companion." I realized I should probably be friends and not lovers with this person.

In other cases, I've been able to check off only "lover," and good chemistry clouds judgment like nothing else! However, I did not feel I could—or even wanted to—confide in my lover as my friend. I knew that good sex was not enough to sustain a marriage and build a life together (though I had to pause and convince my hormones of that fact).

Checklist #3: Must-Haves and Can't Stands

You must distinguish your needs from your wants and your preferences from your absolute deal breakers. You may *prefer* someone who is over 6 feet tall, but you realize that you have more important must-have characteristics in a partner. (My friend Dan is 5 feet 8 inches and used to be frustrated that women online wouldn't date a man shorter than 5 foot 9. He said, "Would these same women be disappointed if someone who looked like Jude Law or Tom Cruise walked in for the blind date?")

I like people to confine the "must-have/can't stand" list to five items in each column. That way you can stay open minded and not limit yourself by trying to follow a long laundry list.

Name five things you *must have* in a mate and five things you *can't stand*. It can be as silly as wanting your partner to dance or

as serious as wanting to be with someone of the same faith. Whatever is important to you, write it down. In some cases, one side
will reflect the opposite quality of the other.

If you are simply repulsed by bald men, list baldness as a can't
stand! You are entitled to some deal breakers—even superficial
ones—when looking for your future mate.

One of my clients volunteered to share her must-have/can't
stand chart:

MUST-HAVE	CAN'T STAND
Generosity	Self-centeredness
Humor (he understands mine, too)	Lack of motivation
Self-awareness	Arrogance
Family values	Sense of entitlement
Chemistry (I want to kiss him)	Argumentativeness

When you consider men you have dated in the past, did they
fulfill your must-have/can't stand list?

When you are forced to really focus on what's most important
to you, you will more clearly identify the kind of person you would
like to date.

We must stop doing things because we've always done them,
shoulding all over ourselves with our romantic choices. And we
must stop using superficial checklists to find a husband.

Use your must-have and can't stand list as a blueprint in dating.
And remember: Find a man who respect and reflect your values;
appreciates your passions; and acts as a good friend, partner, companion, and lover.

Exercises

1. Discover what you are passionate about and commit to it. What's one step you can take this month to get closer to your passion? Write it here:

_____

_____

_____

2. Imagine the kind of guy you would like to be with. What is he passionate about? Where might he hang out? Brainstorm at least five spots

1. _____
2. _____
3. _____
4. _____
5. _____

Dating Dare

Include "He must be really into me" as one of your five must-haves. Those six words will automatically affect your dating success.

4

What Is a Soul Mate?

When American novelist William Wharton's daughter Kate met the man she would marry, she called her father to ask. "What is love?"

Mr. Wharton answered the deep question very simply, "As far as I can tell," he said, "it is passion, admiration, and respect. If you have the two, you have enough. If you have all three, you don't have to die to go to heaven."

There are countless classical, spiritual, contemporary, and highly personal definitions of the term "soul mate." Spanning back to ancient times and across the globe, people have searched for the kind of deep and transcendent love that is thought to join two souls for a lifetime and beyond. Poems, plays, and other great literature on this topic continue to mystify and inspire us.

Yet when our grandparents and great-grandparents wed decades ago, marriage served far more practical purposes. Until the 20th century, the Western model of marriage was centered on an economic arrangement between two families, with an emphasis on producing new bloodlines to support a community's population. (In fact, for many years the Catholic Church didn't officially recognize a marriage if the couple was unable to conceive.)

Our great-grandparents may have grown to love one another, but chances are their marriages were to some extent arranged by others, and they probably didn't give much thought to whether or not their spouses were also their soul mates.

You may have family members who to this day are eager to set you up with the more desirable bachelors in your community (especially if your ethnic or religious background dictates that you marry within the culture), despite the fact that you are uninterested in those candidates. These likely well-intentioned but often misguided relatives probably appear to be baffled by your resistance. When you don't want to date these men, you are often labeled "too picky"—or, in my friend Jillian's case, "lesbian."

Many of the women I interviewed who paired off with their NTs believe that their partners are their soul mates. These women admit that even though they did not initially consider their NTs to be romantic matches, they almost instantly felt a level of comfort and connection that was unusual and even extraordinary.

I believe it's possible to have more than one soul mate in this world (and if you're anything like me when I was single, you'll probably think you've met him each time you visit Brazil or France). The odds are that you will come across at least one person in your lifetime who stirs your soul. So remain open, stay aware, and be present . . . he is looking for you, too.

The First Soul Mates: According to the Kabbalah

The idea of a soul mate is intrinsically linked to the idea of destiny. How often have friends advised you that romance will happen with a man "if it is meant to be." In fact, many religions propose that our mate is preselected in heaven and it is our job to find him.

Throughout my life, a number of Jewish grandmothers (otherwise known as "bubbies") told me to have faith that I would meet my *beshert*—or soul mate—one day. A few years ago, just before I walked down the aisle as a bridesmaid at a good friend's wedding, one bubbie remarked, "Don't worry, Andrea, you'll meet your *beshert*, too, but it takes work to find him." I know Bubbie X was trying to comfort me, but my smile had disappeared the moment she told me not to worry. (Don't you find that you worry more when people offer unsolicited advice like that?) It was difficult enough to find someone I really clicked with, I thought, and now I was supposed to track down just one person God intended me to be with?

I never really understood what the word *beshert* meant, so I recently asked Rabbi Shlomo Zarchi, one of the country's top scholars on Jewish mysticism (Kabbalah), to shed some light on what Jewish tradition says about soul mates.

For one to understand the Jewish perspective, Rabbi Shlomo said, she has to start at the beginning (literally the beginning!) with Adam and Eve—the first soul mates. In Hebrew, *Adom* (Adam) means "person"; so Adam was neither male nor female— Adam was both. The male side and female side were on the front and the back of the same being. God knew that both sides needed to face each other to be whole, so he split Adam and Eve in two. It was their job to find a way to face each other and to become one again. Every union repeats the same story of creation, Rabbi Shlomo explained. We are together with our mate in heaven and then broken apart. Our job in life is to find our soul's other half.

Beshert is a Yiddish word that translates as "intended one." Its origins come from the Talmud (the series of oral and written records that cover Jewish law, ethics, history, and customs). The Talmud states that 40 days before a baby is born, God decides whom that person will marry. In fact, according to the Talmud, much of our lives is predestined. Before we are in this world, God determines who will be wise and who will be foolish, who will be rich and who will be poor, who will be our parents, who will be our children, and who will be our intended mate, or our *beshert*. The only thing that is not predestined, according to Jewish custom, is who will be virtuous and who will be wicked. We have free will—and this is where Rabbi Shlomo said that courtship becomes complicated.

With free will, we are sometimes blind to the fact that our intended soul mate may be right in front of us. When he is presented, we may be driven by other desires that have to do with material power or ego, or we may be unready for a commitment. These factors can cause us to miss him altogether.

I believe that sometimes we look so hard to find our intended mate that we sabotage both ourselves and the potential to connect with someone wonderful. It is the great paradox of the dating process. If you stay at home alone and watch your DVR every weekend, you are guaranteed to stay single; but if you are obsessively looking for your ideal match, you are not fully present and may put unnecessary pressure on the courtship process (which a guy can sniff from 50 yards, trust me). You may miss the men you actually could connect with because they do not fit the image you had in your mind.

My friend Esther married her NT, Shachar. He's a great guy. While she wasn't unattracted to Shachar, she more or less dismissed him when they first met "because Shachar did not fit the story I had in my head of the man I would marry. What's funny," she told me, "is that the guy I pictured in my head was my future husband's friend! I met them both at the same event and hardly noticed my husband because he was an accountant (boring!) and really not my type."

Esther's response touches on a theme that I've heard from women who have paired off with NTs but almost missed their partners because they held on to a certain image of who their soul mate was supposed to be. These women felt that they would know their match when they *saw* him. They didn't consider that they would know their match when they felt what it was like to *be around* him. All of the women admitted that the NTs they ended up with had a powerful effect on them, drawing them in and inspiring them to feel like a great version of themselves, even though they may not have realized it was a romantic connection at the time.

Esther now knows how unfortunate it would have been if she had closed the door on her husband that night. Knowing Shachar's friend now, Esther finds it funny that she initially believed he was the right match for her. When she started speaking with Shachar, however, Esther instantly felt a connection. She was completely engaged by their conversation, and Shachar became sexier to her the more they spoke.

Think about how many times you may have potentially closed the door on a suitable mate because he didn't match the story you had rehearsed or the preconceptions you held.

We've all heard that "you find someone when you're not looking," but the reality is that when you are single and interested in getting married, you are looking on some level. I just believe that many women are looking in the wrong places. In the case of an NT soul mate, it is not that you find him when you are not looking. Rather, it is that you find who you are not looking for.

Rabbi Shlomo told me that there is a saying in the Talmud that for God, matching people is as difficult as the splitting of the Red Sea. I wondered: Is it that much of a miracle to find our soul mate? "It is!" exclaimed the rabbi. (Just what you needed to hear, right?) He continued, "Imagine how much God wants two people who are meant to be, to be together—but he has to keep them apart—like holding the water of the Red Sea apart—until the timing is right. With free will and all the choices we have, sometimes we make poor decisions that lead us off track."

So if the timing is wrong or if a woman is not open to seeing her match, God has to start all over again and find a new soul mate for her. (The rabbi also said that God may have created this world in 6 days, but he has spent all his other days finding us love matches. Turns out God is the biggest matchmaker of all!)

It takes maturity and wisdom to recognize our purpose on earth. Our authentic self is sometimes lost. If we are not aligned with our calling or our most authentic selves, then God's process of matching us is also derailed. It is at this point, the rabbi told me, that God has to work with who we have *become*, not who we were intended to be when our match was first made. This made sense to me as a relationship expert who encourages women to get aligned with their values and passions before hoping to attract a suitable life partner.

Why would God put us through this exercise if we were predestined to be with a mate? Wouldn't it be easier to start together or get clear signs of whom we are intended to be with? That way we could prevent all the crazy crushes, unrequited love, and hang-ups over our ex-boyfriends. Why would God make so many of us so confused in the process?

The rabbi answered simply: "Because the Kabbalah teaches us that two halves becoming one is more unified than just starting with one. The act of reattaching is much more powerful than the two halves would be if they had never been split." He compared it to mending a broken bone; the bone becomes stronger when it is fixed. "To take something that is perfect and complete and find a way to make it even greater is much more powerful than what you had in heaven when you were one. When these souls reunite, their connection is more passionate and emotional."

This made sense to me, too. After all, someone who has never suffered through the pain of a broken heart may not feel the depth and power of true love when she finds "the one." The process of looking for him may be frustrating at times, but the rabbi says it is meant to challenge us.

Power, ego, and material or superficial reasons may conspire to keep you apart from your intended mate, but Rabbi Shlomo and I want you to listen to your soul.

Your Other Half: According to the Ancient Greeks

Each of us when separated, having one side only, like a flat fish, is but the indenture of a man, and he is always looking for his other half.

—*Plato*, The Symposium

When men wore togas and women sported gladiator sandals (long before the trend appeared on the sidewalks of New York City), the concept of having a soul mate was a popular topic of debate and discussion.

It's believed that Plato was the first philosopher to publicly address the idea of soul mates. In his play *The Symposium* (or "dinner party"), each character ponders the meaning of love. One of the main characters, Aristophanes, reinforces the idea of finding your other half when he tells the others at the party that each human was originally designed to be a perfect creature consisting of two faces and all the parts of a woman and a man, but Zeus feared their power and split them all in half. Each person would then spend the rest of his or her life searching for their other half.

Perhaps influenced by biblical teachings, Plato's writing reflected the idea of two souls reuniting. He called the blending of two souls an "ancient need" and wrote, "And when one of them meets with his other half, the actual half of himself . . . the pair are lost in an amazement of love and friendship and intimacy, and would not be out of the other's sight, as I may say, even for a moment."

Aristotle's definition of *soul mate* differed quite a bit from that of his teacher, Plato. My friend Karen Salmansohn, who has studied love from the perspective of Greek philosophy and frequently writes and lectures on the topic, credits Aristotle as the person who first brought the idea of the soul mate to the world's attention. If there were a trademark for the term *soul mate*, Aristotle could claim it.

To understand Aristotle's philosophy about happiness in a relationship, Karen said, we must first look at what he said about happiness in general. Aristotle taught that one of the main reasons people are unhappy is that they mistake pleasure for happiness. Pleasure is about the stimulation of the body and ego, while happiness is about the stimulation of your soul—Karen called this the "G-spot of happiness." It is unlikely Aristotle talked about the G-spot per se over 2,000 years ago, but he did offer a framework about love that applies to modern-day relationships, broken down into three main categories:

Relationships of pleasure. These are relationships characterized by excitement and living on the edge—the flings you have that are about sex, drugs, and rock and roll. Aristotle said that because these unions are superficial and exist on the surface, they cannot bring true happiness.

Relationships of utility. Those in utility relationships use one another to garner status, power, beauty, fame, or money. The trophy girlfriend and sugar daddy stereotypes fall under this category. This is about what another person can give you, and these relationships are driven by the ego.

Relationships of pleasure and utility are all about body and ego; therefore, Aristotle said, they cannot truly stimulate your soul. There is only one relationship that brings true happiness to the people involved in it—the relationship of shared virtue—which captures the true meaning of *soul mate.*

Relationships of shared virtue. These unions are about being with someone who challenges you, inspires you, motivates you, and supports you to become your best possible self. This relationship is one in which you look for someone who intimately understands the real you and helps you live up to your potential. Aristotle explained that relationships of shared virtue nurture your soul and are the real deal (my words, not Aristotle's).

Aristotle's shared virtue is similar to my shared values precondition of a successful relationship. Both convey the idea that when you are with an authentic match, you rise to become the most authentic person you can be.

"You Complete Me"

We've all heard a husband call his wife his better half. We've also heard people talk about their desire to find "the one." And now we know that the origins of these expressions are, however indirectly, derived from ancient sources.

I remember sitting in a movie theater in 1996 watching *Jerry Maguire* and hearing the audience's collective sigh when Tom Cruise's character professed his love to Renée Zellweger's character by declaring, "You complete me." For years after this line was uttered onscreen—and still today—people all over the country have quoted "You complete me" in wedding speeches and Valentine's Day cards.

I can't say that I found much inspiration in Jerry's line, nor have I ever dreamed about hearing those three words from a lover. Waiting for someone to complete me seemed like an unhealthy idea. I felt that I was more likely to fall in love and find a life partner—or a soul mate—when I was complete and balanced, not broken or waiting for someone else to make me feel whole.

I believe a woman finds lasting love when she is happy and living a life aligned with her passions. As an added bonus, a woman is more attractive to potential mates when she is living passionately while being open and excited to meet a partner who may enhance her already wonderful life.

I once worked with a 32-year-old woman who wouldn't take her dream trip to Italy until she could share it with a man. She couldn't remember a time when she didn't have the desire to explore that country. In fact, she minored in Italian in college to prepare for her dream journey. Over a decade later, her language skills had become rusty and she still hadn't made the trip because she felt the experience wouldn't feel right without a man beside her. "It's such a romantic country—I want to share it with the love of my life," she said. I suggested that going to Italy while she was single didn't have to preclude a trip to Italy with her mate later in life. She and her future husband could certainly travel there together and see cities or sights that she wouldn't have time for in her first visit. She could share a wonderful new experience and a fresh new perspective on the country with the person she loved. I also reminded her that waking up to her passion would reignite her life and therefore respark her dating life.

You may guess by now what dating homework I gave her: *Go to Italy!*

After working through her initial resistance (and her gremlins, who said, "You can't go to Italy now! That's not responsible. . . . You should just go to Florida and see your folks instead!"), she took 2½ weeks and explored the Tuscan countryside, the rich history of Rome, and the charm of Venice. She ate the best pizza of her life in a small mountain town near Milan (where they made fresh cheese!) and fell in love (well, lust) with a new man almost daily.

She returned from her trip with a sexy, post-Italy glow and a renewed sense of confidence. She has been dating more than ever and admits now that she can't imagine why she was waiting to meet someone before seeing that magical place.

Similarly, I met a woman in one of my workshops who told me she was waiting to open a special bottle of wine until she could share it with her true love. She said, "We'll toast to each other, and it will be very romantic!" I asked her, "Is this the only bottle of great wine you will ever drink?"

A month later, she shared the bottle with three girlfriends on New Year's Eve. Before they headed out to a party, they toasted the great year to come. "After all that build-up, the wine wasn't even that good," she told me afterward. "But my friends and I had a lot of fun that night!"

And there's my friend Cathy. She spent years hating her cramped, bedbug-infested apartment, but she said, "I need to hold on to it until I meet a great guy and can move out and move in with him." I never understood her logic. She was waiting for a guy to build a great home with, but how would she get close enough to someone if she couldn't even invite him over to her place?

Eventually, Cathy had had enough of her roommates (both the woman she lived with and the bugs) and decided to move out. She bought a cute home and decorated it in her favorite color, pink (the place looked like Barbie had broken in to decorate). Cathy was thrilled with her dream home and loved her new kitchen (and her new pink Cuisinart!). She started to host dinner parties and told friends to bring other single friends. At one of her parties, she met a great guy whom she subsequently married. He professed his commitment and love to Cathy, but with one condition—that they repaint some of the rooms or find a new home to build together. Cathy ultimately moved in with her husband, but she may not have met him had she not followed her passions and lived her life fully—without waiting for a man to complete her.

Women on the other side of the spectrum—those who say they want to get married but believe there is little room for someone to influence or deepen their life experience—may face another issue. Few men want to date a woman who doesn't feel she can learn or grow from a relationship. Men (like us) want to believe that they can add to and enhance their partner's life, and that life together can be even better than they could have envisioned alone.

It's great to look forward to the day when you can create a home with your lifelong mate, and it's important to think about how someone you love can fit into your already wonderful life. But waiting for someone or something else to "complete" you keeps your life stuck on Pause or Fast Forward instead of tapping the momentum of Play. And life is certainly more fulfilling on Play.

Why It's Important to Fall into Like

I can't count how many times I've spoken to a woman who knows that she's in an unhappy, unhealthy relationship but stays in it because she 'loves' the person. I'd guess it happens about every second in America. Every second a woman out there makes excuses to herself and to her friends about why she is going back to or staying with a man who isn't the right match for her and justifies it with the L word. "I know he's been a jerk, but I *love* him!" or "He told me he loves me, so I'm going to try it again. . . ."

I love *love*. I write about love. Love is a beautiful, powerful, and essential emotion for all of us to experience. I don't think you should marry anyone whom you do not *love*. But I'd like to add another critical L to your relationship vocabulary: LIKE. Like is an underrated and hugely important component in relationships.

Many of us take Like for granted because we don't experience the same drama or angst with Like that we may have experienced with the ever-powerful force of Love. Like does not make us overlook some potential red flags or cloud judgment in the way that Love might. Like glides in when you are not looking for it. Like is natural and easy.

I like that Like is simple. When we like someone, we rarely spend hours analyzing why that is the case—we simply accept that we enjoy being around the person and want to spend more time with him or her. When we do not like someone outside the context of dating, we usually just avoid spending time around that person. Somehow, though, when we are romantically linked to someone we don't particularly like, we give in more easily because of Love or the other powerful L word—Lust.

Studies show that women fall in love more emotionally than men do. Research conducted by biological anthropologist Dr. Helen

Fisher demonstrates that when women are falling in love, memory regions in the brain are active, which may be one reason that women are more likely to fall in love with men they already know and when they least expect it. With a nontype, sometimes feelings of love are borne out of a very simple and easy experience of deeply liking the person. For this reason, we should all pay close attention to those we fall into like with.

Most of the women I interviewed who ended up with NTs could not picture being in love with their partners—they just knew that they enjoyed being around them. They were not pressured by Like as they might have been with Love, so they were present and honest in the relationships and romance blossomed.

When you start hanging out with an NT who intrigues you, invite Like into your heart. Do you like who he is? Do you like yourself around him? Do you like experiencing the same things in life as he does? Are you so in like with him that he is one of your favorite people to be around? If you answer a resounding yes to all of these questions, you may be falling into like. And don't be surprised if love follows.

How Do You Define a Soul Mate?

As part of the survey I conducted with OkCupid.com, I posed the question "What is a soul mate?" The responses I received were even more varied than I'd anticipated. Here are a few examples:

"When you can read each other's mind without even looking at each other."

"Someone I connect with mentally, physically, emotionally. Someone I have that chemistry and click with. No matter how much time we spend together, I want more."

"A soul mate is the person who completes your life and makes every day worth living. Your soul mate still gives you butterflies after you've been together for 50 years."

"I don't believe in soul mates. I find the entire concept laughable, really."

"Someone you feel a connection to. Almost as if you have known him all your life. A comfortable, familiar energy."

"I'm not sure. I guess I'll know when I meet him."

"A soul mate = pure crazy love."

To me, a soul mate is someone who complements—not completes—me. How do *you* define a soul mate?

Looking back at our ancestors' ideas of a soul mate, most definitions capture the idea that connecting with our intended mate is a heavenly process—one that we must not sabotage with the distraction of worldly concerns. Many of these sources suggest that there's one person in this world for each of us. While I'm in complete agreement that a higher power or the universe steers us toward the right people in life, I'm slightly uncomfortable with the idea that there is only one "right" individual to merge your life with. I believe that throughout life, you will connect with a number of people who will inspire you and help you grow—and if you are looking to settle down, you will discover that some of these people are more suited to be long-term mates than others. I do think that when you meet someone who "gets" you, the connection you share with the person often feels like you are operating on another level—a spiritual plane. Sometimes your best girlfriend can feel like a soul mate, and sometimes you meet a soul mate on vacation and know in your heart that the experience is meant to

The Five Soul Mates

I once met someone who'd heard that each of us has five soul mates: spiritual, primal, emotional, intellectual, and "the one"—the latter encompassing the four other elements. If we find any of our five soul mates, she said, we are lucky. Perhaps she made this up (in my research, I could not come across the source—so bonus points if you can), but I found the framework interesting. Haven't we all come across people—men and women—who have inspired our soul on a deep level and fulfilled us in very different ways?

stay there. I believe that a soul mate can have many different manifestations, and I like the notion that we can intersect with soul mates at various points in life.

When I dated men in the past, I did not know what a soul mate was, but I knew what a soul mate was *not*. I knew that feeling misunderstood, frustrated, or confused with a partner probably meant that he was not my lifelong match or my soul mate. I knew that trying to convince a person of my worthiness or trying to convince myself of someone else's worthiness was not the stuff of true love. I knew that whatever a soul mate was and wherever a soul mate appeared, the connection would feel organic.

Even though I did not have romantic feelings toward Michael when we first met, I did experience a deep level of comfort— almost like a deep, intuitive knowing—that he would be in my life in some way. It seemed like I already knew him. I just figured he would be in my life as my friend. Most of the women I've interviewed who eventually fell in love with NTs admitted that they were drawn to the person long before they realized what that may have meant.

Feeling pulled in an organic and visceral way toward someone you do not know, especially when that person is not your type, is the opposite of following a checklist full of superficial, "great catch" criteria. You may not be able to explain the feeling or the comfort level you feel with the other person, but you recognize it as something special and perhaps even extraordinary.

When you are dating an NT, your connection with him—and the fact that you feel so at ease with him—often transcends your own logic or other people's judgments about why he may not be a suitable match. It's difficult to ignore the realization that "this guy gets me" or the feeling that you want to share more with him. In this case, your gut may convince you to explore a relationship with him, even if your head remains unconvinced.

Ultimately, if the idea of finding a deep and soulful connection with your future mate is important, you may not be able to resist following your heart and embracing your nontype once you feel a special connection with him. You will want to know him more.

I asked Rabbi Shlomo if there is any way we can know definitively when we've stumbled across the person who is our soul mate. "There are certainly litmus tests," he responded. "According to the Kabbalah, you realize you are with a match when you are not focused on what he can do to make your life better. Your reasons for being with him are centered around self-love." In other words, you are not looking for some kind of validation and are not focused on external gifts (power, money, or other ego-driven pursuits). Rather, Rabbi Shlomo explained, "When you are with a soul mate, you have an overarching desire to attach to that person.

There is a certain selflessness that happens when you are connected on this level—the person drives you to be more giving. A
soul's natural tendency is to transcend from the material world to
the spiritual."

The goal must be to find the depth of a connection that you
believe is timeless, sacred, selfless, and soulful. When you feel this
authentic connection, you don't even have to understand it—you
just have to acknowledge it. This is a soul mate.

Dating Dare

Interview a friend or family member who seems very happy
in her relationship. Ask why she believes her relationship
works so well.

Part II

The Nontypes

A Note on the Nontypes

So what's a *nontype* anyway?

Depending on the person you talk to, the definition of a nontype (or NT) varies. If you are usually drawn to younger guys, an older man may be your NT. If you are generally attracted to edgy guitar players, your NT may be a clean-cut, conservative businessman.

Note: A man who is physically or verbally abusive should be ruled out by all women. He should never be any woman's type.

NTs come in all kinds of packages. For this book, I have chosen a few classic nontypes that my clients invariably refer to as the kinds of men they would "never" consider dating. These men are generally not cast as the lead characters in romantic comedies (unless they are written into the script as comic relief). They are rarely found in the dating scenarios single women daydream about. These guys are often ruled out because they make less money, don't live up to a woman's physical ideal, are of a different ethnicity or faith, are too young or too old, or are just friends. They may be off limits because they work in the woman's office or live in a distant city or are divorced.

Think about the NT men that you may have ruled out in the past or have heard your friends dismiss. Who has been on your "never" list and why?

The popular television show *Sex and the City* incorporated many story lines with NTs. In fact, the series finished with three of the four main female characters in commitments with men who were unlikely matches. There was sophisticated and sassy Samantha, who found true intimacy with someone almost half her age; Miranda, the uptight lawyer who married a goofy blue-collar guy from Queens; and prim and proper Charlotte, the beautiful WASP, who married a chubby, balding, and brash Jewish divorce lawyer named Harry. All of these characters were surprised by their choices, but the audience believed that they had found happiness with these men. It was not the story line we expected, but when these women paired up with their NTs, we experienced the same "good match" feeling that Charlotte eventually had when she told Harry he was the man for her.

The Three Classic Nontypes

I have divided the NTs into three main categories:

1. **Departure nontype (DNT):** He possesses the opposite qualities of the kind of person you usually like and date.
2. **Superficial nontype (SNT):** He doesn't add up on paper and is rarely on any woman's perfect-spouse checklist.
3. **Circumstantial nontype (CNT):** He may have many of the qualities that you're looking for, but his circumstances prevent you from making the leap.

You may meet a nontype who falls into more than one category, and this will further confuse your feelings for him. I hit a grand slam with my husband. On a superficial level, he didn't have the kind of career that I expected my mate would have; our circumstances were complicated (I was living in the United States and he was in Canada); and he was also my friend.

All the women you will meet in Part II paired off with DNTs, SNTs, and/or CNTs. All were surprised by their romantic matches and thankful that they'd followed their instincts to give their partners a chance. Considering that this book is all about dating against your type, it's only fitting to dedicate substantial space to the three NTs and the women who have dated them.

5

The DNT: Departure Nontype

Nontypes (NTs) come in many varieties. If you find yourself smitten with a man you never imagined you'd like—he is an NT. When you start looking outside your comfort zone and find a man who is the *opposite* of your usual type, he is what I refer to as a *departure nontype* (or DNT). If you usually date extroverts, your DNT may be an introvert. If you generally love artsy, bohemian types, the DNT you click with may be more comfortable in a suit.

The DNT is proof that if you keep dating the same kind of men over and over—something's not working. It seems like an easy enough equation, but it is difficult to change behavior that we believe will make us happy.

In this chapter, we'll meet women who were surprised to find themselves drawn to their DNTs—but who found lasting love by opening their minds to the possibility of dating someone who seemed, at first glance, to be the opposite of their type.

"He's Too Nice"

As I conducted interviews for this book, I came across women who said they had never considered nice guys to be their type before they married them. This sad perception is all too common. So let's take a closer look at this particular NT in case he sounds familiar to you.

My friend and colleague Lisa coaches people in dating, but she always had trouble following her own advice. She recently married a man named Luis who is nothing like the kind of man she used to date. She admitted that when they first met, she hardly noticed her future husband. He was different from the men she was typically attracted to. One of the main reasons? He was nice.

According to Lisa, "Luis was totally not my type! First, he looks so young. Second, he's my height. And third, he seemed too nice for me. Can you believe I actually thought that? The guy was too nice for me? Well, back then, if the guy was too emotionally available, I considered it a weakness."

After Lisa broke her dating pattern (one in which she dated unavailable men who did not know whether or not they wanted to commit to her), she realized that being with a nice guy—who was also available for commitment—was liberating. "With a nice guy, there are no games," Lisa explained. "There is no wondering *Does he like me, is he mad at me?* There is no self-induced torture, no *If only I was thinner, prettier, more his type.*" She added, "Being with my nice guy is easy, fun, and fabulous. I get to be me, no apologies."

Lisa is so compatible with her husband that she can hardly believe she resisted Luis's interest at first. She and Luis made plans to go out the weekend after they met, but she flaked and forgot about the date. He called her out on it. She remembers being surprised that a nice guy could challenge her. "I liked that Luis didn't put up with my crap, so I agreed to see him," she said. "Once we had our first date, I knew I'd be a fool not to let myself get to know this nice guy. Maybe he wouldn't be 'the one,' but wasn't it worth finding out more? I decided to give him a chance, even though he wasn't my type, and accept him. It was the best decision I ever made."

Another life coach I know, my friend Cynthia, had a similar experience. Before she met (and married!) her current partner, Gerald, Cynthia rarely dated men who were emotionally available or who treated her well. She did not have the confidence to believe that she deserved better than a man who disrespected her.

"My type used to be bad boys—men who treated me badly . . . party-hard types and players," Cynthia admitted. "A nice guy was good for my best friend. Not for me. I thought nice didn't attract attention. Bad brought attention. I craved the attention. I confused attention with approval. Being noticed meant I mattered.

"When Gerald and I first met, we were not attracted to each other. We were colleagues and got to know each other through social events. He was the geek and I was the party girl. We became friends. He was my Sunday-morning brunch buddy. I would tell him all my dating nightmare stories. Then he asked me out on a date. It was my 33rd birthday, and I was inexplicably nervous! I knew then my heart must have a mind of its own."

Unfortunately, over the years I have met too many women who shared Lisa's and Cynthia's attraction to bad boys. I'll never forget one bright, single 38-year-old woman who told me that being nice and being interesting are mutually exclusive. She did not want to be bored with her mate. I asked her if she was nice and interesting. "Of course I'm nice—but it's different with men," she said. (Don't these statements look even more ridiculous when you see them in writing?)

Cynthia was once able to relate to this unhealthy perspective. "I think women view nice men as weak. We love to know someone is strong, powerful, and in control. There is a sense of wanting to be dominated yet respected."

The issue, of course, is that if you equate nice with weak, you will have a hard time respecting or feeling turned on by the "nice" available men you come across. Repeat after me: *Nice* and *weak* are not synonymous!

Here's another common theme I've heard from women who are drawn to bad boys: They'll change these guys and help them rise to their potential. This is one of the biggest and most common mistakes women make in love. I know a woman who often dates fixer-uppers and then wonders why they disappoint her after all the time and work she has put into helping them. Entering a relationship with a man you want to change—or who needs you in order to change—is a recipe for disaster. In any healthy relationship, you and your partner help each other to become the best version of yourselves; you enhance one another's lives. As I mentioned in Chapter 4, people are best positioned and most ready for a relationship when they feel whole and complete. If you feel you need to rescue a man because you see him as *broken*, or if you want to be the woman who changes a man's unhealthy dating pattern, you are setting yourself up for disappointment.

Whatever their reasons for getting involved with bad boys, these women usually later admit that the initial excitement of a mysterious, hard-to-catch guy was soon replaced by frustration and resentment. As one woman expressed it: "The price you pay when you share your life with someone who is unkind or selfish is simply too high for the perceived excitement this kind of person brings into your life. The never-ending drama is simply not worth it."

When you avoid the nice or good guys, you can expect many more years of bad luck in dating. And in the meantime, you're sending the absolute wrong message to the absolute right guys. Do you know how many men tell me that they feel they need to act like jerks to attract women? They see bad boys getting all the girls and modify their own behavior accordingly, playing games to attract the women who would otherwise not give them a second glance. Be mindful of the messages you are sending to the men around you.

When you take a hard look at your dating pattern, do you find that you're generally attracted to men who are a challenge? Are you generally the pursuer or the object of pursuit?

One of my clients told me that she didn't feel comfortable letting men pursue her because it gave them all of the control. The irony is that she, in fact, has *less* control when she tries to control a situation. When she calls a man many times a week or cyberstalks him ("So he doesn't forget about me!"), she is creating exactly what she fears—a man who will lose interest quickly.

Oftentimes, single women ask me whether a guy they've been seeing for a while is really interested. They'll relate every detail of their conversations, including things he may have mentioned about the future. Hopeful, they'll ask me, "He talked about the future. That must be a sign that he's into me, right?" I usually respond by asking the woman to tell me what the man is *doing* now (not a week ago or when she first met him) to pursue her.

Pretend your dating life is a silent movie. Rather than deconstruct everything the guy you are dating says to you, start to look at what he is *doing*. Is he making an effort to see you often? Does he call when he says he will? A man communicates his interest in a woman through his actions—both *on* the date and *between* dates. Ask yourself, "What kind of effort is he making to ensure I am comfortable, treated well, and happy?"

Bottom line: If you are dating someone who does not put in a lot of effort to be kind to you—move on! If you are dating someone who is unsure about his feelings for you—move on! If you are dating someone who likes you but says he is not ready to be with you exclusively and *you* are ready for a serious commitment—move on! You will not convince a man of your worthiness by accepting his disrespect or his uncertainty about your value. In fact, one of the biggest turnoffs for a man is seeing a woman stick around after he has been rude to her or hasn't called her back. After all, would you want to be with a guy if he stuck around after you treated him poorly? Lack of self-respect is simply not sexy.

If a man likes you, he *wants* to pursue you. Let him. I realize that's an easy thing to say about an issue that can be complicated.

So why would a girl pursue a guy who's not interested in the first place? She might be insecure and feel confused or turned off when a man offers positive attention; she may not be ready for commitment and intentionally or even subconsciously may choose men who are not available; or she may like the perceived excitement of a good challenge and the thrill of the chase when a man is difficult to catch.

I've often heard single women complain that a guy must be a phony when he is too nice. I remember meeting a super-friendly and interesting guy at a party with one of my girlfriends last year. When the guy left to get us a glass of water, she complained that he was trying too hard. This man struck me as sincere and sweet.

Some women are so jaded by guys who have treated them poorly that they do not believe there are any good guys left. Carrie, who attended one of my workshops, told me that she'd sabotaged her relationship with the last nice guy she'd dated because she'd wanted to hurt him before he had a chance to screw her over. She was certain he was a game player like the rest of the guys she had dated. Unfortunately, this guy wasn't playing a game, and after he realized Carrie was, he broke up with her. When Carrie later realized that her fears had overtaken the relationship and prompted her to treat him with disrespect, she begged him to give her another shot. He was no longer interested.

If you get turned off when a man is turned on by you, ask yourself why and explore those feelings. You must challenge and change this pattern if you truly want to find your mate.

Get out a pen now and list 10 reasons why any man is lucky to be with you. If you need help, recruit a girlfriend to help you flesh out the list. You may be tempted to flip the page of this book, but give this exercise your best effort!

Ten reasons why a man is lucky to be with me:

1. _____
2. _____
3. _____
4. _____
5. _____
6. _____
7. _____
8. _____
9. _____
10. _____

If you have been treated with disrespect by a guy you have dated, ask: Why do you think you have tolerated it? Your response may reveal a deeper issue that you may decide to examine with the help of a professional.

"He's Too Clean Cut"

Rachel is a 30-something woman I met in my cardio kickboxing class in New York last summer. I overheard her talking to another woman in class about her upcoming wedding to a guy named Colin who was "so not" her type. I could not help but barge into their conversation and ask a million questions based on that one statement. (Lately this is my problem—my antenna goes up when I hear "he wasn't my type.")

Who was her type before her fiancé Colin? "I think my type was anyone who seemed dangerous, out of my league, exciting, rugged, a little bit raw, adventurous, funny, spiritual . . . the kind of guy that my friends and family hoped I would never date," Rachel said. "I was attracted to hippies, long hair, grizzly beards, ripped jeans, mountain bikers, Birkenstocks, go-where-the-day-takes-you sort of attitude. Or I was attracted to another type: shaved heads, tattoos, motorcycles, rebellious nature, noncommittal, nonconservative types. I loved artists. I loved guys who were really into music. I don't think I ever knew to date someone for an actual 'future.' I dated for fun, for a good time, out of physical attraction, out of pure lust, greed, selfishness . . . and I usually dated men who had the same reasons for dating."

When Rachel first saw Colin online, she thought the way he wrote was cute and he looked cute. "But when I saw him on the street in person, I was afraid that he was too clean cut for me. His shirt was tucked in, and he had a sort of all-American look to him. He played baseball, had been in a fraternity in college, and worked on Wall Street. These things rounded out the equation for the kind of guy I preferred not to date."

What changed? When did she realize she was interested in getting to know Colin better? When did she know Colin was her

DNT? "During our first date, I was caught up in the moment, surprised at how well we got along, how easily our conversation flowed, and how attracted I was to him, despite his impeccable grooming," Rachel said. "I know he looked at me and thought that I looked all wrong for him in my tight jeans, heels, and low-cut shirt."

Rachel acknowledged that the checklists she had previously used to find a boyfriend or husband had limited her choices. Her so-called requirements were not the criteria that would likely lead to a happy or lasting relationship. "I think that even when two people get together because they think that the 'type' is a perfect fit, they run into problems. I would have differences with whomever I was in a serious relationship with," she explained. "Many women I know are still single because they are holding out for a specific type of man. When we create this outline for what type we want, we set ourselves for someone we haven't even met or fallen in love with—someone who doesn't exist."

Today, Rachel feels bad for women and men who are constrained by arbitrary criteria, as she used to be. "There are so many things that could keep two people apart," she said, "but you have to ask yourself how important these *things* are versus how important this *person* is. How do these preset qualifications measure up against the person in front of you?"

Rachel has a point. Looking for a mate is not the same as searching for a great apartment or job, where you may refuse to settle for less than highly specific criteria like high ceilings and plenty of closet space or health insurance and a short commute to work. You can envision how you want your perfect home to look and probably furnish and fix it to match your picture of it. Relationships and chemistry are more complicated because people are more complicated. You cannot predict how someone will act or how you will feel with another person. And when you exclude so many of the possibilities based on types or extensive lists of desirable traits, you're limiting your chances of finding a mate. Look at the man standing beside you. How do you feel? Are you inspired? Annoyed? Excited? Confused? Curious? Attracted? The person you meet may not be your type *and* you may be completely drawn to him. It happens all the time.

"He's Too Much of a Rebel"

My friend Natalie lives with a DNT. He is nothing like the kinds of men she had dated in her 20s, when she preferred clean-cut, conservative men. In fact, she married one of these "perfect" guys when she was 28.

"I was married to a wonderful man who I thought was my type," she recalled. "He had many qualities one would look for in a good catch—he was smart, kind, and a good provider. My family felt comforted that he would always take care of me."

Even though Natalie is a passionate person, she was not passionate about her fiancé. But she figured that she was probably expecting too much. She was with an amazing person whom most women would be thrilled to marry, so she knew she *should* marry him. She looked at the facts: Great guy—check. Good job—check. Nice family—check. She enjoyed spending time with her man, and he treated her well, so what was there to question?

Natalie now admits that when she married this man, her instincts were numbed and her head wasn't clear. "I was at a point in my life where I was cut off from what I really wanted or who I was. Because of this, I did not make good decisions. When you are not living authentically, your decision-making process becomes strained."

Natalie and her husband were opposites—she was an overly emotional and passionate extrovert, and he was a cerebral introvert. Many couples like this make a relationship work when their values are similar or when they are not threatened by their differences. However, in Natalie's case, her husband favored sticking with a routine, while she preferred—and very much valued—exploring the unknown. This caused tension and discontent in the relationship.

Natalie did not initially realize that she was missing the kind of connection that she now has with her NT, Dale, and did not realize how love could feel. Today, she feels more like her passionate self.

"Dale has this strong and intense personality. He wears his emotions on his sleeve. I had never dated or been in a relationship with someone like that in my adult years. He is totally open and completely emotionally honest. I value those qualities tremendously."

I asked Natalie if she recognized the importance of these qualities once she divorced her ex. She laughed and told me that she didn't really know what she was looking for until he was in front of her. She had known Dale when she was much younger (they met at camp). Dale had always found Natalie cute, but the teenage Natalie wrote in her diary: "I can't stand Dale! He repulses me. I'd be happy if I never had to speak to him again!"

The two reconnected online a couple of years after her divorce. Natalie was intrigued by their exchanges and surprised that she looked forward to Dale's e-mail every night. Still, she did not think it would lead anywhere, "at least consciously," she admitted.

But when she and Dale reunited in person, she realized that what made Dale "repulsive" in the past was now one of her favorite traits.

"He pushes me in a way that I haven't experienced in a romantic adult relationship. You see, there are different ways to push someone, and not all are positive. Dale was never pushing me to upset me or to compete with me. He was pushing me to be my best self. I realized it was nice to have someone truly challenge me. I had not had that in past relationships with 'perfect' men who were 'my type.' "

"He's Too Introverted"

"When I hang out with an introverted guy, I feel like I've taken an express bus to Yawnsville"—that's how my childhood friend Debbie used to describe what it felt like for her to date men who weren't outgoing. The funny thing is that Debbie was never the life of the party. When we attended events together, she would cling to me as if I were her social lifeboat. When she said, "Who are we going to meet?!" it always meant, "Who are you going to introduce to me?!" I realized that Debbie felt like a yawner herself when she wasn't around outgoing personalities.

Extroverted people irritated Debbie (she complained that they were too pushy); intimidated her (she would get quieter and more shy around them); and inspired her (she told me she wished she could be as naturally social and fun as they were). When Debbie was alone with close friends like me, she was engaging and interesting; but when Debbie was in public with extroverts, her personality shrunk and she preferred to follow rather than lead a conversation.

Debbie once dated a guy, let's call him Loudmouth, who lectured those around him about everything from where to buy real estate to why we shouldn't get the flu shot. Loudmouth was a sports agent and I felt like I was part of a competitive game of *who can get a word in* during every discussion with him. I'd try to participate in or ask questions during his rants and reviews, but I never felt that he really heard or cared about anything I had to say. Loudmouth actually raised his voice when people tried to interject in a discussion with him so that he could dominate it. It was exhausting to have a conversation with Debbie's boyfriend as he spoke *at* us—never to us.

Loudmouth is an extreme example of an extrovert who is oblivious and insensitive to those around him. I am extroverted but I also like to *listen* to others in a conversation. I genuinely enjoy learning about other people. Many extroverts I know are outgoing and thoughtful; but Loudmouth was not one of those extroverts.

The fact that Debbie, who used to get embarrassed when asking a waitress a question, gravitated toward men like Loudmouth was odd but perhaps not completely surprising. It's common to see couples in which one person does most of the talking. The issue I had with this guy was not that he talked more than my girlfriend did, but the fact that I didn't recognize her when she was around him. She deferred to him for everything (which might have been okay if their values were similar), and she did not exhibit the shining personality that her friends knew and loved. When Debbie and Loudmouth attended events together, I noticed that she crawled even further into her shell. *She* became the dreaded yawner.

When Debbie said dating introverted guys was like taking the fast lane to Yawnsville, I contemplated what track she would be on with a guy who was a little more understated—a guy who was not her type. I wondered how Debbie's personality would show up when she could not rely on the man she was with to provide the evening's entertainment. What would happen when the spotlight shone on Debbie, without anyone to jump in front of her?

Then two years ago, after ending things with Loudmouth and

joining an online dating site, Debbie met a quirky and witty writer named Sam. Sam shared Debbie's love of 1950s Americana. He also wanted to travel to Machu Picchu. Debbie and Sam e-mailed each other a few times before making a plan to meet for drinks. She imagined that Sam would be boisterous and entertaining, just as he had appeared in their brief e-mail communications, and she could hardly wait for the date. However, after their first date, Debbie was concerned. Sam was much quieter and more reserved than she had imagined. She said, "He asked me all these questions about myself!" as if it was a problem. She told me he put her "on the spot" and complimented her smile. "Isn't that weird?" she asked. "It's refreshing!" I told her. I asked Debbie if Sam bored or annoyed her (since I do think that if someone irritates you early on, it may be a sign that he is not a match), but she told me that was not the issue. She liked spending time with Sam, but dating him was outside of her comfort zone.

I'm sure by now you can imagine the punch line to this tale: Debbie and Sam are a great couple. She moved in with him almost a year to the day of their first date. Being around them, it is clear that Debbie is a really authentic and happy version of herself. She speaks up more than she used to and asserts herself in social situations. I asked her recently if she noticed that, too. "It's so funny how I thought it was an issue that Sam cared enough about me to want to take the time to learn about my interests and values and really listen." She reflected on it, "It felt strange at first to have all the attention on me . . . but he understands me really well and because we are both shy, I find that being with him has helped me to speak up. I've learned a lot about myself." In other words, being with the right partner helped Debbie rise to her potential.

What about the generalization that introverts are boring? "Boring!" she laughed. "Sam is one of the deepest, wisest, and coolest people I have ever met!" She added, "You know, just because people are shy, it doesn't mean that they're dull. A lot of introverts are interesting," she remarked, forgetting that it was her—not me— who once had the "no introvert" rule.

We generalize about what an introvert or an extrovert is like and make dating decisions based on our assumptions. I've often heard women say, "I would never date a guy who wasn't outgoing" or "I hate guys who want to be the center of attention." Sure, there are extreme examples of introverts and extroverts who would be difficult to date, but there are plenty of people who fall somewhere between the two ends of the spectrum. I'm a very extroverted person (I never took my mom's advice not to talk to strangers), but I love taking long walks alone with my music and I prefer to write in solitude. Michael is introverted by nature but he is a fantastically funny and outrageous improv performer. When he's on stage, I marvel at his ability to put himself out there in a bold and unpredictable way.

Most people are multidimensional and cannot be summarized in such simple terms. Don't assume that the guy sitting in the corner at your friend's party is dull, uninteresting, or uninterested in you. If you are irritated by extroverts, don't peg the guy buzzing around the room at an event as insincere or "trying too hard." One part of dating an NT is staying open and making decisions about people on a case-by-case basis.

"She's Not My Type!"

My former classmate from journalism school, Vicki, found perhaps the biggest DNT—or departure nontype—of any woman I interviewed for this book. She left her husband and eventually pursued a relationship with her current partner, a wonderful woman named Lisa.

I remember chatting with Vicki at the end of the school year. It was months before her wedding, and she was dreading the idea of wearing her wedding dress as she walked down the aisle. It would make her feel uncomfortable, but she said she'd wear it to satisfy everyone else. I remember her advice to me—I was listening closely, since she was getting married and I figured she must know a lot about successful relationships: "Andrea, you don't have to be ga-ga in love when you get married. You just have to ask yourself: Can I live with my man's most annoying habit? If the answer is yes, he's good to marry."

I quoted Vicki often through the years before I met Michael. I would tell people that "ga-ga" is overrated and fleeting, so it was silly to expect that. Vicki had a practical way of looking at marriage, and I appreciated her view. After all, I thought, electricity fades over time. As long as you are not annoyed with your partner, you are doing well. I felt this was a good way to measure what was right.

Years later I discovered that when Vicki had shared that wisdom with me, she had been quoting friends who were trying to comfort her when she had cold feet about marriage. Vicki told me that most gave her "well-intentioned but terrible advice like 'I loved my husband when I married him, but I wasn't *in* love with him.' Or 'There's not always a spark like in the movies.' "

In the months and weeks before her wedding, Vicki was miserable. Everyone kept telling her how happy she should be—must be—would be. Loved ones and strangers told her how lucky she was to land Mr. Right, who was smart, handsome, and funny and who had a great job. Even though Vicki's gut was screaming for her not to walk down the aisle, she convinced herself that *she* was the problem and pushed on.

Vicki recounted the day she got married: "My mother and father drove me to the church. When we approached the parking lot, I screamed for my dad to keep driving. We drove for about 20 minutes, right out of the city limits. I was in the backseat, hyperventilating, while my divorced parents squabbled in the front. After much debate, we turned around and returned to the church, where I got married. It was the saddest day of my life, and I didn't know why."

Vicki says now that she didn't realize what kind of love was possible in her life until she met her current partner, Lisa, at work.

Vicki really liked Lisa but didn't give a second thought to having a relationship with someone of the same sex. "Lisa was the girl on the second floor at work, and I just thought she was the best—pretty, smart, funny, totally charismatic," Vicki recalled. "She used to have my job, and I'd find myself wandering upstairs to ask her questions about the position. That soon turned into me looking for excuses to visit her. I didn't really have words for what was happening, but I knew I loved being at work—and hated being at home."

About a year after Vicki's wedding, she divorced her husband. "It wasn't a sudden epiphany—it was a slow realization that I couldn't 'be in love' with my husband. Once I realized I was gay, it all made sense. All those Indigo Girls albums, my *Buffy the Vampire Slayer* collection, baseball caps, and soccer league. Geesh, I was a walking stereotype! It was months after the divorce was finalized that I finally had the nerve to ask Lisa out."

As with all of the other women who fell for NTs, Vicki's feelings crept up on her until they were undeniable. Vicki had the same confused reaction experienced by many women who fall in love with an NT: first, confusion and fear at the thought of pursuing a

relationship with someone she *shouldn't* like, followed by excitement and comfort that she had a romantic connection that she
had not even realized was possible.

Vicki knew on her first date with Lisa that she was going to
marry and grow old with her. "It was like in the movies and is still
to this day. I feel giddy when I get home from work and see her.
All along I was trying to fit with Mr. Right, when Ms. Right was
waiting for me on the second floor."

Discovering one's sexuality, as Vicki did, is certainly a different process from simply realizing someone is not your type.
However, the theme of following your gut and pursuing someone you like, even when he or she may not add up on paper or
be in your usual frame of reference, is a good lesson for all of us
and is the sentiment shared by all of the women I spoke to who
found love with NTs.

6

The SNT: Superficial Nontype

Filmmaker Judd Apatow has created story lines with many NTs who do not look like leading men but still manage to capture our hearts as they awkwardly get the girl. There's chubby and goofy Seth Rogen in the 2007 hit *Knocked Up,* who plays the leading man to beautiful Katherine Heigl, and geeky and uncomfortable nice guy Steve Carell in *The 40 Year Old Virgin,* who pairs up with smart and sexy Catherine Keener.

The *superficial nontype* (SNT) is the guy who is rarely on *any* woman's checklist. He doesn't feel like an immediate match when you first meet him, because he is too short, too tall, too skinny, or too fat; has bad hair or no hair; is a bad dresser; doesn't make enough money; or just simply seems *wrong* for you at first glance. Simply put, this NT may not inspire immediate chemistry.

The SNT possesses some of the most important qualities you're looking for in a mate but falls short in some of the external qualities that you generally imagined your future husband would have. When you realize you have feelings for this nontype, you surprise yourself—you may have thought you were more superficial than you actually are! This should be good news, but it momentarily freaks you out. You realize that you have to let go of the image of the perfect-looking man if you are to be with your SNT, but you are willing to do so because of how you feel around this person. What you used to find icky—like running your hands through a thinning hairline or kissing a guy who meets you at eye level—doesn't seem like such a big deal once you've fallen for this man.

It Just Happened

Many years ago, my good friend Lahna called me from Texas.

"Andrea," she said, "I think I've fallen in love." I was confused, since she sounded more pensive than happy. She told me this man was wonderful . . . "and he's really fat."

"So he's a bit pudgy . . ." I began.

Lahna interrupted me: "He's 600 pounds."

Slim and gorgeous Lahna had become friends with Ralphie. They met at an open mike night in Houston, where Lahna was performing comedy. Ralphie was visiting town and was already established in the comedy circuit. He told Lahna she had great potential, so they decided to keep in touch. "It didn't even occur to me to date him," she said. "I don't know if it occurred to him either. I don't think either of us thought it was realistic or possible, even though there was something special the first day we met."

In the months following, Ralphie and Lahna spent many hours on the phone developing a close friendship while Ralphie mentored her. It was during this time that Lahna fell for him. It just happened. "I went out to Los Angeles to visit him after all these phone calls. I knew I really liked him, but I couldn't imagine being physical with him."

What changed? "I just felt drawn to him when we saw each

other again," she explained. "He was so caring and so confident. Once he kissed me, the sparks flew, and he gave me butterflies."

I have heard similar stories from many women. Sometimes, they say, they didn't even realize how attracted they were to a particular man until he made a move. The feelings crept up on them.

To make Lahna's situation more challenging, Ralphie was of a different faith and didn't have a lot of money. Lahna knew her parents would be concerned that Ralphie was not a "safe" option, but she also knew she'd never felt so in love with a man.

Lahna's story is an extreme example of pairing off with an SNT, or someone who doesn't look like the person most women imagine marrying. But Lahna's concern about Ralphie's weight went beyond his external appearance. Lahna is one of the most fit women I know. She kicked my butt when we took a boot camp class together, and she loves to hike and bike around Laurel Canyon in Los Angeles. Being healthy and physically active is part of Lahna's lifestyle.

So how does Lahna handle the fact that she and Ralphie can't share many aspects of the active lifestyle she enjoys? Lahna reminded me of my own advice—that a good partner appreciates and respects your values, even if those values are not his own. "Sure, I wish Ralphie could be as physically active as I am, but he gives me so much to be happy about that it's not as much of a sacrifice as I thought it would be. I hike with friends, and I take long walks with our dogs. I don't miss out on doing the things that I love just because he can't always participate."

Ralphie has also taken great strides to get healthier and lose weight in the years that he and Lahna have spent together. Early in their relationship, Lahna expressed her concerns about how his weight impacted his health. She assured him that she would do what she could to help him reach his goals.

Lahna's situation is not the same as that of a woman who dates a man she intends to "fix," even though the man is not privy to her makeover plan. In Lahna and Ralphie's case, Ralphie *wanted* to change, and he felt that Lahna could help him get there. Some women might not be able to make this kind of commitment, but Lahna and Ralphie had such a strong foundation from the beginning that she was happy to stand by his side and help him achieve his goals.

Today, Ralphie May is one of the country's most successful comedians. He headlines all over the nation, performs for our troops, and hosts his own special on Comedy Central. Lahna is his opening act and a successful and accomplished comedienne in her own right. Since Lahna and Ralphie fell in love, he has lost almost 300 pounds and now makes great money doing what he loves (and what he is amazingly talented at doing). He credits Lahna for much of his success. Lahna's career has also taken off. She realizes that being with Ralphie has given her professional and personal life more focus and meaning. Both know that they would not be where they are now without each other's support and love. They embody the idea that when you are with the right match, you rise to your best potential.

The amazing thing is that even if Ralphie had not found financial success and fame or lost half of his body weight, I know my friend Lahna would love him just the same. He brought out the best in her and makes her smile every day. Ralphie was Lahna's perfect NT. Their two kids are pretty cute, too.

Me, Michael, and Money

One-third of working women in the United States outearn their husbands. Yet in the survey I conducted with OkCupid.com, almost 82 percent of the women polled said they would consider dating a man only if he made more money than they did.

I hate to admit that money was once a factor in my own dating life. I like to think that when I was single, I was open to all kinds of men regardless of their paychecks. In reality, I had pictured myself marrying someone who would earn a good living so I could sustain the quality of life I had grown accustomed to. This was not always conscious. If you told me then that I only wanted to be with a man who earned good money, I would have responded that a guy's earning potential was *not* my most essential must-have. (I know many other women who also say this but don't truly believe it.) It's not that I felt I needed material goods like fancy shoes or designer dresses, but I am a glutton for interesting experiences, and many of the ones I enjoy—live theater, traveling, and fine dining—are more easily accessed with some dough.

When I was trying to figure out if I should keep dating a great man (who also made a great salary) or risk following my gut feeling to be with Michael, one of my friends asked, "Who would you rather be in a foxhole with?" Good question. The guy who made good money would get us out of the foxhole, so I chose him. (I've recently realized I have a hard time answering questions about what I'd do in situations that involve a desert island, a foxhole, or being secluded with one person in some other way. It doesn't seem romantic to me to be cut off from the rest of the world—or my iPhone.)

My friend rephrased the question. "You are *in* the foxhole. You can't get out. You have to stay in it with one of these guys. Who are you going to be with in there?"

"Michael!" I blurted out. I was surprised at how easily I picked him as my foxhole mate.

"Why did you choose Michael?" my friend asked.

Without thinking, I said, "He would make me laugh every day. He would make our little foxhole the coolest one in the neighborhood, and he would protect me every night. Hands down, Michael is the guy I want to be in a foxhole with more than any man I know."

Less than a year after this realization, Michael and I moved into a 350-square-foot sixth-floor walk-up apartment in New York City's Greenwich Village. When I noticed that I couldn't unpack all the plates (it's hard to unpack kitchen items when an apartment doesn't come with counter or cupboard space), Michael hugged me and welcomed me—and us—to our tiny abode. He told me how much fun we would make it and how wonderful it would be because it was our little place to create together.

In the past, I had thought I'd feel most secure with a man who made enough money to provide me with a great home. I know now that *home* is so much more than a nice big structure. I never imagined I would feel so excited, comfortable, and peaceful in such a small space. I was at peace because in my heart, I knew I was in my foxhole with the right person. Even with such little closet space.

I recently met Debra, a successful entrepreneur and single mom. Before marrying her current partner, who is a public servant, she dated type A business guys. At 29 years old, she married one of these men, who held a top position at a financial institution. She soon realized that when her husband was not entertaining clients and impressing his colleagues at work, he was unstable and selfish and had an alcohol problem. "I now realize that my ex-husband liked me when I was a depressed, unhappy law student and lawyer," she said. "As soon as I switched into marketing and started to do really well, things went downhill."

Debra's ex continually put her down by saying things like

"Don't tell people you're a vice president; it makes me look bad." He often told her, "I know the meaning of the word *compromise*; I just choose never to do it."

Debra stayed in the marriage for 3 years. Even when her gut instinct was to leave, she always let other people convince her to stay and work it out. After all, they reasoned, he was a great catch.

Debra felt that her friends expected her to pair up with a career-driven man because of her own professional ambition. For years after her divorce, she continued to date ambitious, business-minded men who made a lot of money.

One day Debra stopped and thought about how completely different her friends were from the men she chose to date. Her friends were witty and well rounded and had full, rich lives outside of their jobs. The men she dated were, well, difficult. "Since I have a natural talent for dealing with difficult personalities, I never really noticed how difficult these guys were when I was dating them," Debra said. So she shifted her perspective and got clear on what mattered most. "It's all about priorities. Do you pick your friends based on their earning potential?"

With this change in outlook, Debra started to view people differently. One day, she was driving home and passed a man painting the fence in front of a modest house. She thought to herself, "I need a guy who would paint his own fence, not hire someone to do it." (This is the funny thing about switching your perspective — you can see something every day and hardly notice it until you've made a conscious mental shift.)

The next day, she met her future husband at her son's school open house. He was a single parent and someone she might have previously overlooked because of his lack of professional ambition. "We spent the first month sending lengthy e-mails back and forth, talking much in the way my girlfriends and I did (about kids, books, TV, relationships, etc.)," Debra recalled. "We liked similar things, had similar priorities. It shocked me that while I had lots of guy friends like him, I had never dated anyone like him."

And how did it feel to date someone who was not her usual type? "I purposely dated him *because* I realized he was exactly the opposite of what I had been dating!" she exclaimed. "I did have one overlapping date with a type A business guy, and it only made me realize that this was not the kind of relationship that I wanted. It was clear from the outset with the single dad that we were in an equal partnership."

Debra describes her SNT husband as a type B guy who has his priorities in the right place, and whose biggest priority—their four children—aligns with what's most important to her.

She proudly adds, "And yes, I knew early that he would paint his own fence! In fact, together we painted the entire interior of his house before my son and I moved in."

Dating Down

Over half of the women who took the OkCupid.com poll admitted that they have never dated a man shorter than themselves. Many single women list a man's height as a deal breaker.

Even though my parents didn't understand why I strayed from my type when I first started dating Michael, they should have seen it coming. After all, they have their own unconventional love story.

My dad, a refugee from Hungary, did not resemble anybody my mom had previously dated or been interested in. My mom was 5 foot 9, and my father matched her toe to toe on a good day. At first glance, though, most people thought my dad was shorter—and this was initially a deal breaker for my mother. After my dad asked for her phone number, my mom told her girlfriend, "I'm certainly not going to wear flats at my own wedding, so it can't go anywhere."

Knowing my parents, I find it hard to imagine why my mother would have passed on the opportunity to be with my father. I suppose it felt foreign to date a shorter man. Ironically, though, his "foreignness" eventually became his main draw. My mom realized that my father's close-knit family (who had escaped from Budapest), his enthusiasm for food, and his passion for music and culture were qualities she wanted in her life.

Would You Date a Shorter Man?

- Fifty-one percent of women polled in the OkCupid.com poll said they would not consider dating a shorter man. Some of their reasons included:

    "I don't find short men remotely attractive. It's unlikely I'd ever fall for somebody shorter than me."

    "Height is not of great importance, but I like my men manly, and I can't imagine a manly man who's shorter than I am."

    "I feel safer with a person who is taller."

- Forty-nine percent of females surveyed said they would date a man a few inches shorter than themselves.

    "Height is trivial compared to intelligence, humor, and other valuable characteristics."

    "Height really doesn't matter; it depends more on how attracted I am when I first see them."

    "I would normally say no, but the person I'm interested in at the moment is a little shorter than me."

My mother told me, "I realized that maybe the framework I was used to—the circles I was moving in—weren't truly who I was or what I valued on a deep level." My mom felt more interesting around this interesting man! (Remember: It's not just who the man is. It's who you are *with* him.)

Did the height issue disappear? She said she stopped thinking about it when other things became more important. For her wedding day, however, she did make concessions. "I got a pair of low heels in white satin," she recalled, laughing. "A few days before the wedding, I went to the shoemaker, who cut off the bottom of the heel. Oh—and I slouched."

This short story has become a long and fruitful marriage. The funny thing is, as my mom has gotten older, her annual physicals have disclosed that she has shrunk a full 2 inches! My dad is now taller than my mom.

That's a true love story.

My college friend Christine recently married her SNT, Matthew, an old friend who is about 3 inches shorter than she is. It is easy to be shorter than Christine, as she stands at 6 feet, but she had always dated men over 6 feet tall and pictured her husband at that height, too.

Early in her friendship with Matthew, Christine told me it was a shame that Matthew was shorter than she was, since he seemed perfect for her in so many ways. She felt comfortable around him; he was one of the funniest guys she knew. "Just sort of short," she explained. "I had always envisioned myself with a man who would tower over me, as I had always associated that with a feeling of protection."

But as Christine got to know Matthew over the years, she realized being with a tall guy doesn't necessarily mean you'll feel safe with him. That may sound like a simple insight, but to Christine, it was a powerful realization that helped her see her friend Matthew in a whole new light. "I dated some men in my early adulthood who were just slightly taller than me, and they always hated when I wore heels. With Matthew, though, I realized that I didn't need to adjust myself to make him feel better."

Matthew loves everything about Christine, including her height. He loves when she puts on high heels and struts her stuff. "His confidence is such a turn-on and makes me feel better about myself, which then becomes a turn-on. . . . It's a nice circle to be stuck in," Christine said with a huge smile. Talking to her, you can tell she feels like the sexiest and sassiest version of herself with the man she married.

The love checklist Christine had previously been using, with height as a must-have and other criteria that didn't equate to long-term fulfillment in a relationship, seems silly to her now. "Good looks fade, six-packs soften, and bank accounts can be so easily depleted. Ladies qualify successful matches by qualities that don't equate with relationship longevity," she said. "What women should be looking for is how that person makes them feel about themselves. You have to be at a certain place to be open to that kind of love. If you are willing to take on the burden of what other people think, then you will not see the wonderful person in front of you. You will be too preoccupied worrying that someone will look down on you for dating a guy who is shorter than you."

Christine's solution to worrying about others' negative opinions about an SNT? Repeat this mantra: *Who cares what you think? He makes me feel good!*

7

The CNT: Circumstantial Nontype

The final nontype category, the *circumstantial nontype* (CNT), describes a man who possesses many of the qualities you seek in a mate, yet is someone you might automatically consider to be off limits or too risky because he lives in another city or country, is of a different faith or background, is divorced, is an office mate or friend, has children, or is older or younger than you. Because of his less-than-ideal circumstances, the CNT is someone you probably never imagined you would date. When you are drawn to these men, the shoulds that you thought you had tamed may come back to haunt you.

Many people believe that dating should be convenient or easy. How many times have you heard someone say, "I just knew it was right—everything happened so naturally!" But real life—and real love—is rarely storybook simple.

It can be tough to align the feelings in your heart with the thoughts in your head, not to mention the realities imposed by real life. Many times we can be too quick to invoke the practical or logical terms of relationships right at the start, even though pragmatism is not always the best quality when it comes to matters of the heart. We rule out so many possibilities of love simply because we fear that outside circumstances may conspire to make the relationship too much of a challenge. But CNTs, like any other NT, are worth a second look and an open mind.

Flying High in Love

I once had a client named Heather who received a lovely e-mail from a cute guy on the online Jewish dating site JDate.com. She was excited by the guy—until she realized he was writing to her from Uzbekistan. What made the story especially thrilling for Heather was not the fact that she was contacted by an attractive and eligible bachelor, but the fact that there are still Jews in Uzbekistan.

Like many people, Heather thinks it's impossible to initiate a long-distance relationship—whether the person resides in the former USSR or another part of the United States. And many more believe long distance doesn't work, period. I understand where these people are coming from—it can be hard enough to maintain a relationship with a man who lives in the same city. But I believe that to find success in dating, we all have to take risks. If you feel a connection with someone, I think that's worth exploring. After all, who wants to wonder for the rest of her life if that guy on the plane might have been *the* guy?

I was involved in several long-distance relationships before I married Michael. In fact, I was planning to give a shout-out in my wedding speech to my credit card's air miles program, because I was certain I'd end up with someone who was from a different part of the country. For years on my birthday, friends and family members donated air miles to my cause!

When I was in my 20s, I met a man at a Bay Area concert while I was visiting from Toronto. He and I enjoyed a geeky and very postmodern courtship on e-mail before I decided to move out to northern California to give our relationship a real shot. Five years later, we broke up, and I did not leave my heart in San Francisco. But I don't believe the relationship's end had anything to do with the way it began. I never regretted making the move or taking the leap to see what would happen. I knew that if I didn't give it a chance, I'd always wonder *what if*, and I thought he was worth the investment. I knew *I* was worth the investment.

Not everyone is as comfortable hopping on a plane for a date or relocating for love. My friend Jill once told me that she would be perfectly content to stay in the same city—in the same neighborhood where we grew up—for her entire life. Jill is a deep person who prefers a simple lifestyle. She embraces routine. Feed her the same few dishes for dinner every week and she'll be happy. She doesn't need to rock the boat; she values stability and gravitates toward a lifestyle that supports that need.

A few years ago, Jill was having a rough week in Toronto. I suggested she take advantage of discounted airfare to New York and visit me for the weekend. "I know cute guys here!" I added as incentive.

Being the crazy matchmaker that I am, I organized an outing with my buddy Brian, the kind of man who gets along with everyone and treats women with the respect Jill was missing in her love life at that time. Within an hour of meeting, Jill and Brian were playing footsie under the table. Before long, I was a third wheel and ducked out early so they could continue their game of foot hockey and prolong their chat. Jill went to sleep at 6:00 a.m. because of her fantastic 9-hour first date. The next day, they made plans to hang out before Jill flew back to Toronto. They talked about seeing each other again.

At first, Jill worried about the inconvenience of dating Brian and the long-term compromises that would have to be made if things worked out. She wasn't convinced the relationship was worth the complications that could follow. She continued to date men in her own city but couldn't get Brian out of her head. I knew Brian was Jill's CNT. I felt there was a strong possibility that they would end up together, because I saw how happy and comfortable Jill was with my friend.

Two years later, I was thrilled to be a bridesmaid in their wedding. I even resisted the urge to say, "I told you so." And no, their story has not been simple or easy. They've had to make tough decisions and weigh what each is willing to sacrifice for the greater good. But according to the once-routine-focused Jill, "Even when we were traveling back and forth to visit each other, I realized that

Traveling for Love

Almost a quarter of the people interviewed in my OkCupid. com survey have traveled up to 100 miles to find love, though close to 65 percent admitted that they would not date someone in a different country. For those who refused to travel for love, most cited reasons like "life and relationships are complicated enough without the distance" or "long-distance relationships never work." The people who favored long-distance relationships said that a special connection does not happen every day, so it is silly to close the door when you find it. "You never know where the love of your life will be," said one respondent. "I wouldn't want to pass up an opportunity to meet someone who could change my life."

Brian offered me more stability than men I had previously dated. There are challenges in any relationship. You work it out when you love and respect each other and communicate—I never regret the risk we took to be together."

Long-distance relationships tend to heighten the best and the most challenging aspects of any healthy relationship. You and your partner have to compromise, you have to communicate, you have to stay connected, and you have to care enough to do what it takes to make your relationship shine. But the time you spend together feels magical, and if you're willing to endure obstacles early on to be with the person you love, chances are you'll be able to weather rough patches down the road, too.

In today's world, long distance isn't the roadblock it used to be—there are so many ways to stay connected. If you find yourself in a long-distance relationship, here are some survival tips.

- **Buy a webcam.** Web cameras are not as high tech or pricey as they may seem, and many laptops come with built-in webcams. Sign up for a free service like Skype (www.skype.com) and see your guy whenever you want! Face-to-face contact will help make you feel more connected. (Just resist the urge to spend the first 10 minutes every night talking about how funny it is to communicate this way—it kind of ruins the romance.)

- **Sign up for a credit card with air miles.** Air mileage will be your best currency when you fall for someone far away. Assuming your interest is mutual, try to keep the momentum by visiting each other one or two weekends a month—or as much as your schedule and your bank account can handle.

- **Don't hibernate when you're together.** Many people in long-distance relationships have a tendency to spend many hours cooped up together when they reunite. Remember: It's just as important to see your partner in his world—with his friends, his family, his interests—so you can make an informed decision about your compatibility. If you have a 3-day weekend planned, use the first night to reunite without an audience. After that, pry your hands off one another and get outside!

- **Live in the moment—even though you're trying to figure out the future.** When you're dating long-distance, you have to plan so much for every date that it may be hard to enjoy the present. It's important to remember there are no guarantees in any relationship. The best you can do is to get to know each other, build together, and have a good time in the process.

- **Don't be afraid of discussions about the future.** As much as you strive to live in the moment, find opportunities to talk about the future. "What if" questions are a natural part of any adult relationship, so don't shy away from them in a long-distance relationship. At a certain point, you'll need to discuss how viable it is for one of you to relocate. If you absolutely cannot come to terms with ever being in the same city, it's better to cut off the relationship before you get even closer.

"He's Just a Friend"

A romantic relationship with a friend is often viewed as off limits or too risky. (After all, who wants to jeopardize a great friendship?) But what if that friend turns out to be your CNT?

How many times have you heard someone say, "I don't see him that way—we're just friends!" and then later learned that the two got together romantically? I hear it all the time. I've said it, too. I'm surprised I took so long to admit that I had feelings for Michael, considering that I'd fallen for male friends in the past. In college, there was Adam, who was one of my favorite guys in the dorm. Adam and I did everything together. He was my go-to guy when I looked for a male perspective, needed help assembling Ikea furniture, or wanted someone to watch bad movies with. When something good happened, it was important for me to share it with Adam. When I was stressed about schoolwork, Adam would calm me. I wanted to be there for him, too. I often visited him with nondorm food (I had this strange desire to feed him), and I was his support when he needed someone to lean on.

After being friends with Adam for more than a year, I realized I'd developed romantic feelings for him (despite the fact that I was dating someone else at the time). Months earlier, friends had asked me if something was happening between Adam and me because we hung out so much, but I assured them they were wrong. I would laugh and explain that just because a man and woman are close friends, it doesn't mean they want to hop into bed with each other. Besides, I told them, Adam was great but certainly not my type. (Foreshadowing?) Today, I can blame my confusion on the fact that I was in college and had not yet learned to listen to my inner voice, but in reality, I repeated this pattern a decade later with Michael.

I recently met a woman named Adriana who had a similar experience. She realized, after many years of friendship with Bill, that she was falling for him. Adriana had originally met Bill in high school, but he was 5 years older than she, and they rarely crossed paths. Years later, they were reintroduced. Although Adriana thought he was cute, they were both involved with other people,

so she did not give a romantic liaison much thought. Bill became
an instant buddy. He was nothing like the kinds of men Adriana
had been dating or was usually attracted to. Adriana liked Medi-
terranean men "with an accent." She grew up with an Italian dad,
lived in South America when she was younger, and lived in Spain
in college. "When I heard other languages, I was instantly
intrigued," she explained. "My friends would say that they knew
they would have to buy an expensive plane ticket to attend my
wedding!"

Adriana loved hanging out with Bill. "We were such good
friends, so I didn't want to ruin it. Bill would date five girls at
once and tell me all about it. I was dating a Brazilian guy, of
course, and would talk to Bill about it. We never wondered why
we were not dating. We were just friends. I was never jealous
when I heard him talk about other women."

Adriana's girlfriends told her that Bill loved her, but she denied
it. Bill was the guy who would help her hang pictures, go for late-
night pizza, be her date when she needed a plus one . . . They had
been friends for years and did not see each other *that* way, Adriana
told them. It didn't occur to her to date Bill, even when she
thought about what a great guy he was. "I remember walking
down the street and talking to Bill on the phone about a girl who
broke up with him. I thought, 'This girl is so stupid! Why would
she end it with him? Why doesn't she see how lucky she is to be
with him?' Even then, it was not totally conscious. I didn't realize
that meant I should probably be with him."

In most cases, when you have developed feelings for a friend,
even if it's taken months (or years!) for them to develop, you usually have a turning point, a lightbulb moment when you admit to
yourself that you are crushing on your buddy. For Adriana, things
changed when her mother became ill. It was a hard time, and Bill

was her rock, the one person truly there for her in her mother's final months. "He would come visit me and my mother," she explained. "I would take care of my mom during the day and stay on the phone with him for 2 hours every night—and that seemed to be my only reprieve. We would talk about life, what we were looking for. Through those conversations and through Bill's actions, I realized our morals and values were in line. That was my 'aha moment.' Suddenly I thought, 'What am I doing?' I started getting scared he would date someone else!"

Adriana initially kept her feelings to herself, but 2 weeks before her mother died, Adriana shared her secret with her. Her mother was supportive. One night after Adriana had admitted the feelings out loud, she and Bill were hanging out with other friends. Somehow things felt different—their exchange was strange, and the tension was palpable, especially when she was flirting with another guy at a party and Bill wanted to leave. He walked her home and admitted that he could not deny his feelings anymore. "I know that everything I'm looking for out there is standing right in front of me," he told Adriana. "I know this is not the right time, but I have to say it." Adriana asked Bill to stay the night. They held each other and kissed. "*That* was the moment," she said.

Adriana's mom passed away soon after that evening with Bill. Adriana wanted to make sure she was not pursuing Bill for the wrong reasons. "Usually courtship is bliss, but ours was hard because of what I was going through. My mom was my best friend, and those months were the hardest of my life. Every day Bill showed me that I had made the right decision to be with him."

Today, she thinks Bill was a gift from her mother. Without her mother, Adriana would never have recognized her CNT. His values make him a perfect match for her.

"You learn about someone's values based on how they treat

their family, how they treat others, where they want to live, how they like to spend their days," Adriana explained. "We don't like everything the same—he grew up with meat and potatoes, and I'm really into food and wine. I think the reason it works is because we are interested in learning about the things that are important to the other. We do a lot of fun things together. We are best friends. Isn't that what everyone is looking for in a husband?"

In the end, most of Adriana's friends did not have to travel far for her wedding: She married Bill back in the town they grew up in. "I married the all-American-looking guy who loves baseball and grew up down the street from me. I never would have pictured him to be my husband, but without a doubt, he's the one."

Work and Play

Another risky romance that may feel counterintuitive (but may be oh-so-tempting!) is one that starts in your workplace. It's no wonder you feel a connection with a certain coworker, since you probably spend the majority of your days in the office and likely have a lot of common interests and experiences.

Most offices have strict rules about office romance and do not encourage it. Your *should* voice may be screaming at you not to get involved with a fellow employee, but your *want* voice may be telling you to pursue the workplace object of your desire—especially if you haven't been this excited about someone in a long time. There are too many happy couples who have met at work, you think, to ignore this CNT possibility.

It is important to do a thorough cost-benefit analysis before you enter a workplace romance with someone who is available (pursuing men who are *not* available is a whole other topic). What are the potential risks and what are the possible rewards of becoming involved with a colleague? Have you reviewed the HR policies about office relationships? Are you in the same department as your crush, or do you and he work in different areas of the company? How will you manage the situation if things don't work out?

If you're attracted to the guy down the hall but don't see a relationship working out long term, it's probably not worth risking your job or your level of comfort at work. If, however, you can imagine a future together, it may be worth the gamble.

Take Kristine, whose CNT, Steve, worked in her office. Steve was a sales rep and Kristine was in management when they met, so she knew she needed to be careful. "I was absolutely terrified when I realized I had feelings for Steve," Kristine said. "I worried, 'What if I approach him and he isn't interested? I'd have to quit my job out of embarrassment! What if we do date and things don't work out?'" But she'd heard only nice things about him and thought he had many of the qualities she wanted in a partner. "Many of the qualities I knew about Steve usually take months to truly understand through dating, but we both had the benefit of 'character assessment' through the workplace and coworkers." In spite of her fears, she was completely drawn to Steve. In her heart, she felt it was worth the risk.

Kristine was the one to initiate contact, calling Steve and asking him out. "I thought about it and realized that *not* making the call would have been worse than having him turn me down and living with the humiliation for the rest of my life!"

When she and Steve began dating, they decided to keep their relationship under wraps at work until they were sure about their future. Her coworkers had no idea they were dating until they announced their engagement. Kristine feels incredibly blessed to have taken the leap.

"I never knew what it felt like to truly be myself in a relationship until I met Steve," Kristine said. "In every other relationship, I didn't feel free to be 100 percent myself. I laughed too loud. I talked too loud. I was embarrassing in public. I'm clumsy and accident prone. Most men would run the other way—but not Steve. Steve would run out to the dance floor and stand over me and say, 'Safe!' like a baseball umpire with his arms straight out while we'd both be crying of laughter."

It is a love that Kristine had never experienced before. The fact that it started at the watercooler is now simply an afterthought.

From Office Mate to Life Mate

As part of my research for this book, I asked people who visited my Web site to tell me about their experiences with office romances. I had a flood of responses, but one woman stood out in particular. Lisa wrote that she dated her office crush, Mark, who was her NT in every way. "He was from a small town, and I was from the big city. He was older than me, and I wasn't looking for a relationship, but we were attracted to each other. We just kept it quiet. No one knew about it except some trusted people. I did ask a couple of people about his reputation and got great responses." Soon after they got together, Lisa left her job for another one— and now she and Mark are happily married. "We've been together for over a decade. Mark makes me want to be the best person I can be. Mark is not only my best friend but my number one fan. I am blessed to have him in my life. It took me a while to figure that out—because he wasn't my type— but I'm so glad I did."

Dating a co-worker always involves some risk. But as you know by now, I'm a firm believer that we all have to take a few risks to find success in love. That said, if you do decide to pursue your office paramour, here are some pointers on managing that risk.

- Do not confide the details of your romance in coworkers, even if you are friends outside of the office.
- Avoid using office resources to communicate your feelings for each other. (That means no sexy e-mails on the company server!)
- Make a commitment to avoid bringing your personal relationship issues into the workplace. If you have a disagreement, work it through off the clock.
- If it's explicitly stated in your contract or the employee handbook that office romance is against company policy, ask yourself: Is it worth losing your job over your crush?

Divorced Dating

Close to 67 percent of the women surveyed on OkCupid.com said they have not dated someone who is divorced, but the majority (58 percent) said they would be open to it. With the US divorce rate holding steady at close to 50 percent, there is a good chance you will meet a few divorced men in your dating pursuits. You may consider a divorcé to be a CNT. In addition to having an ex-wife and all the other complications that ensue with a divorce, some of these men will have children. Before you start dating a single father, you'll need to consider whether you are ready for the responsibility of becoming a stepmother. This is not a decision to take lightly; be honest with yourself before you begin a relationship with a man and his children. Because when kids are involved, you're not the only one at risk of a broken heart.

When my friend Anna was 29 years old and met a man named Michael, she knew he was the divorced father of a 4-year-old daughter. Anna had never dated a single father and didn't know what to expect, but as a divorcée herself, she remained open to the possibility of a relationship. "I didn't want to close myself off from a potentially great experience," she explained. "That's true in dating, and it's true in life in general."

After she and Michael began to talk about a future together, Michael thought it was time to introduce Anna to his daughter. Avery and Michael shared a great bond, and now Anna felt the pressure of having to fit in. Anna recognized that Michael's little girl was his biggest priority and that she could never compete for his attention. "I knew going in that Michael loved me," she said. "But I also knew that I would be second priority in his life, and I had to accept that. That's hard for a lot of women dating single dads. Of course you, as the girlfriend, want to be the most important thing in your guy's life, but you can't be when he has a child. This makes some women insecure—some even compete with the children of their partner.

"Before I met Michael's daughter, I felt a little like I was invading or intruding on this solid bond between them," Anna acknowledged. "I felt like I was this awkward new kid on the playground, a third wheel trying to fit in and wanting to play with them, too.

"The first time I met Avery, I was so scared. I was living in another city, and Michael and Avery came to pick me up. I remember approaching the front seat of the car and Avery motioning to me and saying, 'Sit with me!' I was hooked in that moment. I love her like she is my own daughter now, but there were some decisions I had to make before entering a relationship with Michael and before being in his daughter's life."

Dating a Single Father

When you are dating a man who has children, make it a priority to protect the children's best interests. Consider waiting to meet your date's children until you are sure of the big-picture potential with their father. Similarly, if the man you are dating does not want you to meet his family until things are more serious between you both, try not to take this personally. Be happy that the man you are dating is acting responsibly and thoughtfully before he exposes his children to a new relationship.

While Anna is thrilled to be Avery's stepmother, she advises women who are thinking about dating single fathers to assess their priorities carefully before getting involved. Becoming part of a child's life is a tremendous responsibility. If you're not 100 percent dedicated to the long-term possibilities, it's not fair to anybody. "Kids are kids," Anna says. "I knew that even if Avery didn't warm up to me right away, there was nothing she could do that would make me angry at her. She was a child. I was the adult. Some children may act out when a new person is introduced into the equation—it doesn't matter. When you're dating a single parent, you have to be prepared to not personalize it. It really is not about you—it is about your partner and his children."

Women dating single fathers may also have to shift their expectations about what courtship will look like, Anna added. "Dating someone with kids isn't going to be what one might fantasize about or deem to be the most romantic evening or weekend getaway," she said. "I had to be open to letting our relationship grow and unfold in its own way and to enjoying time together after Avery went to bed or on weekends when she was away. In some ways, our relationship

> ### "Too Old"
>
> Most respondents to the OkCupid.com "What's your type?" survey have dated men up to 5 years older than themselves. And 22.4 percent have dated men more than 10 years older.
>
> The majority of women polled admitted that their cutoff would be up to 5 years older.

unfolded a little slower, but it was also heightened and sped up in other ways because we were playing house! You just can't let that dynamic get ahead of you. It can be great because it really makes the time you spend together about the bottom line—are you a good match? Do your values fit for each other?"

May-December Romance

A 32-year-old woman I met last year told me she only dates men who are between the ages of 30 and 35. Why did she choose those parameters? "A guy under 30 is hopeless, and a guy over 35 must have commitment issues," she said. Another woman told me that the worst age to marry a man is in his early 30s: By that point he has missed the cutoff when most of his friends married, and thus he will not feel the urgency to get hitched until he is older and senses a midlife crisis coming on.

These are the kinds of arbitrary, self-imposed boundaries that limit your opportunities to find love. For every 38-year-old "hopeless bachelor" out there, you can find one who is ready to settle down. A man walking down the aisle at age 38 may have wanted to focus on his career before finding a mate, or he may have been involved in a long-term relationship that just didn't work out.

When it comes to selecting a mate, there are countless theories about age and its impact on a relationship. Certainly your chances of finding common ground with someone who grew up in your era may be higher, but I have met too many women who have found success in dating once they allowed themselves to consider dating their CNTs, including men who were a little older or a little younger than they'd originally thought they would date.

You may remember my friend Madeline from Chapter 2, whose perspective changed about being with Tom, a man 16 years older than she, once she got to know him and became attracted to his maturity and experience. It took Madeline time to adjust to Tom's age and consider him as a romantic possibility.

"We talked for 4 hours straight the first time we hung out, and I hadn't experienced that with a man in a long time," Madeline recalled. "But I had a dilemma: This guy was almost 50 years old! I wondered if it was really possible that I was attracted to him."

Interestingly, when we feel attracted to an NT (whether a DNT, SNT, or CNT), we often question our feelings and wonder if we are just desperate to find a match, since we typically don't go for guys "like that" (whatever "that" is for you). But we rarely question our interest or motivation when we are drawn to our "types," even when there are blatant red flags that our type is not right for us. The fact is, when we fall for an NT, our feelings may be more genuine: We are responding to the actual person, not a type.

Madeline says that when she began to develop feelings for her CNT, Tom, "I decided not to stop myself, and to let it happen. I tried to pace myself, but I could hardly wait to see him a week after the first time we really spent time together."

I think I saw stars in Madeline's eyes when she said, "It was a movie moment when we kissed. He happened to have a stethoscope, and we were listening to each other's hearts. I wanted to make his heart speed up, so I inched in and gently kissed him. It was amazing. When I left, I could not stop thinking about him and wanted to see him again soon. I knew I had to be with this guy, despite our age difference. I thought to myself, 'If Tom's age is your only problem, Maddy, you can work with it. Other people have partners with much bigger issues, like a bad temper or different values!' My only real issue with Tom was that he may die sooner than me—but that was hardly a reason to hold back."

Is age ever an issue now that Tom and Madeline are happily together? "Of course, there's a realization I have that when I'm 45, he'll be 60," she said. "I wonder if I'll be a widow at 65 or 70, and that worries me. But I definitely continue to think it's worth it to have spent that time with him. If our kids lose their father early, I still feel they will be so blessed to have had a father like him.

"I am more aware of Tom's age when we socialize with friends. Sometimes people can be judgmental about it—but I'm an adult, and I have to think about whose life I am living."

It's clear that nothing can make Madeline regret her choice to pursue what she describes as the most fulfilling and mature relationship of her life.

"Too Young"

What if *you're* the older half of a couple? These days, an older woman paired off with a younger man does not have the stigma it once had. Some would even argue that "cougars" (sexy older women who chase younger men) are in vogue, but the women I interviewed who married younger men admit that they were not looking for the age difference. For this reason, these men were their CNTs.

In Chapter 3, I introduced you to Raquel, who made a love connection with a younger guy named Matt at the opening night of her photo exhibit. They married when Raquel was 38 years old and Matt was 33. Although Raquel was instantly attracted to Matt, she worried about how she would feel as the "older woman" if she ever dated him.

"I always wanted to be the cute younger one, but with Matt I would no longer have that prized title," Raquel explained. "He would always be the young cute one in the relationship—and that was a bitter pill to swallow."

I've heard this reaction many times from other "older women." Raquel continued, "I was scared that because I was older, I would be the one to age first, and that maybe he wouldn't find me as attractive when my boobs sagged and my face wrinkled. I guess I was scared he wouldn't love me as much or he would leave me. I think it always comes down to how someone can hurt you. . . . For me, it was the fear that he could leave me."

But it wasn't just superficial concerns that caused Raquel to question her May-December romance. She had to address serious topics, such as her timeline for having children. Many times, older women worry that their younger partners won't be as ready for children as they are. In Raquel's case, it was Matt who brought up his desire to be a dad and expressed concern that Raquel (who was 36 at the time) might not be able to have children by the time they married.

Raquel told Matt that while she understood his feelings, she could not change her age—he could either accept her as she was and move forward, or simply move on and look for a younger mate. "I think because of where I was in my life—happy, confident, and secure," Raquel said, "I told Matt that it was his decision. I needed to feel that he was serious about me. I also couldn't waste *my* time—so this discussion may have felt premature at the time but was an important one for us to have."

> ## Dating Down
>
> According to a recent AARP poll, one-sixth of women in their 50s actually prefer to date men in their 40s.

Over time, Matt affirmed his commitment to her and said he would do whatever it took to build a future and a family together. In the end, Raquel and Matt did have difficulty conceiving a child and needed a little help from medical science. But 2 years after their wedding, at age 40, Raquel got pregnant. She delivered her beautiful baby girl, Margaux, at 41.

What advice would Raquel share with other women who have contemplated dating younger men? "You need to see if he wants the same things that you want, has a time line similar to yours, and has the maturity level to sustain it," she said. "A 30-something woman might want kids in 2 years—and a 20-something might want them in 10. You also need to realize that a younger person doesn't have the experience you have, so you need to be patient. I had a friend who was dating a man 16 years her junior. She was so surprised when he didn't communicate and act like she wanted and expected, so I reminded her that he was only 23 years old. A person's age doesn't necessarily reflect his maturity level, but it does reflect what he's been able to develop within himself. It takes time to learn about yourself, to learn how to make relationships work, and to develop the tools to maintain them."

Like any relationship, dating someone younger boils down to shared values and long-term compatibility. A 28-year-old man is not necessarily less ready or able to commit to you than a 48-year-old bachelor. Consider the individual and what he is willing to give to make a relationship work.

Cross-Cultural Romance

When you fall for a person who comes from a different ethnic or religious background, you may face challenges that seem to exceed those you would face with a man from within your faith or heritage. You may worry about how your family or others will feel about the relationship, and you may feel deeply conflicted when the very things that formed your identity now seem to be at odds with your heart.

As with any potential mate, it's essential to communicate openly, measure how your values align with one another, and determine if the needs of both of you can be met. You may gain much from dating someone who is so different from you and most of the people you know, but you may also risk losing something important to you—such as the understanding or support of your community.

An Interfaith Romance

I've known Ruth since we were girls. She was a few grades ahead of me in school. Through the years I heard updates about her love life from my mother, who was good friends with Ruth's mom. Shortly after graduating from college, Ruth became engaged to the perfect man. He was just about to start medical school. He was everything Ruth (and her family) thought she was looking for.

Ruth said, "I met this wonderful guy while in school, and we were together for several years. My family and friends knew we would be engaged—it was expected. Everyone loved him. He was exactly the kind of person I pictured sharing my life with at the time."

I was surprised and saddened to learn that Ruth's engagement broke off months after her fiancé proposed. Nobody, including

Ruth, predicted the relationship would end. She was heartbroken. After some soul-searching, Ruth decided to spend the following summer on the east coast of Canada, an area that had always intrigued her. She felt calm and focused during her visit there. The following summer she returned—and crossed paths with the man who would change her life.

Ruth met François one night in a small pub on Prince Edward Island. She wasn't sure if she wanted to go to a pub by herself, but she'd heard that the fiddle music there was amazing, and she loved the fiddle. (She followed her passion!) When Ruth saw François on the other side of the bar, he had an aura around him, "almost like a light. I know that sounds strange," she told me, "but I knew I wanted to talk to him, so I sat down near him and his friend and struck up a conversation. We engaged in small talk, and I quickly realized they didn't really speak English! It didn't matter, though. I was drawn to François. I could read how open and friendly he was by his body language and the smile on his face. Fiddle music began playing, and François and his friend missed their ferry home. We were all kind of lost in the moment."

That night, in Francois's broken English and Ruth's high school French, she found out that he and his buddy were leaving for a weeklong camping trip the next morning. He invited Ruth to accompany them, and she accepted without thinking twice.

"I went to the hostel owner that night and asked if I was crazy to join these two strangers. I explained the situation and how excited I was, and the owner encouraged me to go. I think she could see by the expression on my face how much I wanted to go. I wrote down all François's details, his father's law firm contact information, and my info and gave it to the hostel owner so I had someone looking out for me in case I wasn't safe. I don't know, it wasn't logical . . . but I knew I wanted to see him again and join him on the camping trip."

François was French Catholic and 5 years younger than Ruth. "He broke all of the rules," she says. "I wouldn't consider younger guys, and I always imagined I'd marry someone in the Jewish community. I pictured my husband to resemble the people I grew up with."

Ruth was sure she was falling in love with François the next morning on the ferry ride up to the campgrounds. They passed dolphins jumping in the water. It was one of the most beautiful days she had ever experienced.

During their week together, Ruth realized that even though she and François came from such different cultural and religious backgrounds, they shared similar values. They came from similar socio-economic backgrounds, were college educated, and valued their families tremendously. François had an earthiness and authenticity about him that Ruth found refreshing. She fell for him more each day they spent together. It was the first time in the years following her broken engagement that Ruth felt herself again.

When she returned home, she thought about how her family would react to her new love. "My mom had always told me that marriage was hard enough as it is, and coming from different religions makes it even harder. But I remember thinking that her advice was not enough to stop me. Knowing my family may not completely approve but following my heart and pursuing the relationship anyway was strangely empowering," she admitted. Once she felt the soulful and authentic connection with François, she never looked back. "Having my parents accept the man I would be with was certainly important, but my happiness was the most important, and I hadn't been that happy in a long time."

Once others get to know your NT and see all his wonderful qualities, they often warm up more than you could have imagined at first, Ruth said. And if you are close with your parents, it really is true that most of the time, they want to see you happy, she added.

A fiddler played at Ruth and François's interfaith and bilingual wedding—it was perfect, but not anything like the wedding she had been planning the first time she was engaged.

Now that Ruth and François have been married for 5 years, she concedes that cultural and religious differences sprang up the most when they had their first child. But they continue to communicate (he speaks English now!) and compromise to make sure both of them respect the other's position.

Ruth wrote the woman from the hostel on Prince Edward Island a few years ago to let her know that she had married the guy she'd gone camping with. And every summer, François and Ruth take their two children to the campgrounds where they—unexpectedly—fell in love.

Our Authentic Selves

Many of us who are in relationships with nontypes fell in love with our partners by accident. When we spent time with our NTs, most of us were our most authentic selves—bad moods, frizzy hair days, and all—because we weren't trying to impress the people we never thought of as dating material. And our NTs may have also been their most natural selves when they spent time with us, since they didn't feel they had to impress us.

In conventional dating scenarios, you put your best foot forward and keep things light at the start of the relationship. However, when you enter a relationship with a nontype, you often have to face challenges early, and things may not feel quite as simple. You have to weigh what you are willing to give up in order to be with your NT or consider how you will respond to others who may not understand your choices.

Because you face obstacles early, you actually have the benefit of seeing how you and your partner face and work through challenges together. By the time you delve into the relationship and risk being together, you probably will have weathered a few storms together or at least tamed the gremlins in your head. You will know how you and your mate will work as partners, because your relationship has already been tested.

All the women I interviewed for this book admit that the checklists they used to find true love were nothing like the ones they had relied on in the past. Their new love lists were based on mutual respect, passion, common values, connection, and friendship—the kinds of ingredients that lead to long-term fulfillment.

Exercises

1. Think of friends or family members who ended up happy in less than conventional or convenient arrangements. Who comes to mind? What do you notice about their relationships?
2. Have you ever turned down a date with someone you liked because he didn't seem to fit the image you had in your head of what you wanted? Who comes to mind, and what did you learn?

Dating Dare

Log on to your online dating profile and adjust your criteria for height, distance, age, status, and other measurements or characteristics that you usually hold on to as must-haves and that are no longer reflected on your updated love list. Try dating with different criteria this month and see who shows up.

Part III

Step into Action

Creating Change

Why is it that in our culture we seem to be more concerned with "to do" lists than "to be" lists? To borrow a turn of phrase from Deepak Chopra—we're not "human doings."

When you live authentically, you know what to do in life and in love because you know who you are and what you value most. Your expectations and standards are high. You no longer stay in toxic friendships or date men who are unsure about being with you. You don't need to poll 15 friends to ask if the guy you are dating is cute or not. You aren't overly concerned with what "they" say, what "they" think, or what "they" are doing. You realize you are not that important in other peoples' lives—just your own.

In Part I of this book, I encouraged you to think differently about the criteria you use to look for a mate and to get clear on your values. In Part III, we will focus on action. Honoring your belief system isn't just about what you think or say but what you *do*. For change to happen in your life, you have to create it.

I believe there are four critical components of a successful dating equation: taking risks, being present, developing resilience, and just plain having fun. Each of these four components is about taking action and embracing uncertainty. So go ahead—take action. I dare you.

Take Risks

Risk taking is an integral part of successful dating. The uncertainty that accompanies dating may cause you to feel anxious or vulnerable. Many of my clients admit that some of their biggest regrets (which I refer to as "lessons") are a product of being so afraid of rejection that they never opened up and allowed the men they were dating to get to know them.

Here's the irony about intimacy: To attract a partner who makes you feel secure and grounded, you have to surrender control and let your guard down. In fact, I do not believe you can have true intimacy without allowing yourself to be vulnerable. Security and vulnerability can coexist in love.

If you are someone who likes to plan every moment of your life, you probably try to control the way a relationship develops. But if you don't allow someone to see your true (imperfect) self, you decrease your chances for a true connection. If you do not take risks in dating, you will not get closer to your goal of finding a long-term, committed relationship. If you are looking for a short-term fling, of course, your risk-reward ratio is smaller.

In Chapter 8 we will revisit risk, as it rears its head most when you date a nontype.

Healthy Vulnerability

The kind of vulnerability that I refer to doesn't leave you feeling worried or insecure, nor does it make you feel tormented and indecisive. Healthy vulnerability is still scary, but is about allowing yourself to feel exposed in order to ultimately feel understood.

Be Present

Staying present is vitally important. I lived in my head for most of my dating life. I felt that I needed to assess and analyze every angle of every aspect of every relationship. I believed I had to be thorough if I was to make an informed decision. I probably could have written a thesis with arguments and counterarguments about the merits of each man I went out with, whether I saw him once or dated for a few years! Troubleshooting and making projections about our future together was part of my dating process. Today, I am exhausted just thinking about it.

Yes, it's important to consider the realities of life with the person you are dating. We all must be thoughtful about the people with whom we surround ourselves. We must be pragmatic before we enter a long-term commitment. But there is a difference between weighing the realities you face and obsessing over details that you cannot control. Living in the present moment means that you have to give up some control (which has always been difficult for me). It's about going with the flow and being connected to your wants on a very deep and Zen-like level. I call this "yogic dating."

When you are stuck in your head and are not present, you are missing an opportunity to gauge how you *feel* about someone. For instance, a friend recently asked me for advice about a man she was seeing. "I don't know how I should feel about him," she said. I responded: "How *do* you feel about him?" She looked at me like I was crazy.

Many of us overcomplicate answers that would be obvious to us if we just stayed present. This woman was analyzing everything so much that she was ignoring her intuition. I asked, "Do you feel like you want to be around him a lot? Are you attracted to him?

Do you feel like he is the one you want to share romantic and real-life moments with, wake up to, and cuddle up with at night?" She shrugged and said, "Not really. . . ." In fact, I think she had her answer when she had to ask for my advice.

When you are constantly dwelling on what you had in the past or daydreaming about what you want in the future, you cannot enjoy the relationship you are in today. Not to mention that people who are stuck in their heads are much less fun to date or spend time with. Who wants to hang out with someone who can't enjoy the moment?

Being present is the second step to successful dating. If you are not in the moment, there is a good chance that you will sabotage something before you even give it a chance to grow, and you will miss out on how you truly feel (not how you *should* feel) about the person you are spending time with.

Be Resilient

I recently added "resilience" to my successful dating equation because I've talked to so many women who have given up on finding a mate after a series of unsuccessful dates and relationships.

During the dating process, it's normal to feel discouraged when you realize that you aren't the right match for someone who you once thought could be a long-term mate, or when you are rejected by a man who you wish returned your feelings.

As I mentioned earlier, most dates you go on *are going to fail*—that's the inherent nature of dating. That's why it is essential to be resilient and not become too attached to the outcome.

A woman I met at a party once told me that she was angry with a man who went out with her a handful of times and then decided he wasn't interested in another date. She said, "He wasted my time, and I told him so!" I reminded her that this is the nature of dating. During the first few weeks or months of getting to know someone, we decide if we feel enough of a connection to invest more time. Nothing is guaranteed or predetermined, nor should it be. If a man ends a relationship because he doesn't see a future, he hasn't wasted your time—he's respected your time.

Here's a good perspective to embrace: For every person you do not click with, you are one step closer to the person you are meant to find. Staying in dead-end relationships or with men who are not thrilled to be dating you delays your finding a healthy and fulfilling partnership with someone more suitable for you.

I know a 38-year-old woman who has been having an affair with a married man for the past 7 years. (I hope by the time this book is out, she will have finally ended it—though she has been promising to end it for years.) She met him at work almost a decade ago and found that spending time with him was more exciting than actively looking for another man to date. She woke up recently and realized that her biological clock was a few ticks away from age 40. For someone who has always wanted to be a mother, hanging on to a man who cannot commit to her may have hurt her chances of having the family she wants.

Being resilient means bouncing back from dates or relationships that do not work—even those that leave you feeling heartbroken—so that you stay open and vulnerable enough to connect with the *right* person one day. It's about making a choice to believe that the person you are looking for is also looking for you.

If the end of a relationship leaves you grief stricken, by all means cry, sulk, talk to your girlfriends, and heal before jumping into the dating pool again. Make sure you have moved past the hurt of your last relationship before running into someone else's arms. Then turn any regrets into lessons and use what you have learned to go for what you want, need, and deserve right now.

Have Fun!

I end with the fun portion of my dating formula. When you start dating someone new, the connection should feel natural and fun—and if it doesn't, that may be your cue to move on.

Think about what you're like on vacation. One of my clients, Rebecca, admitted that she preferred the "Costa Rica Rebecca" version of herself that appeared when she relaxed and had fun on a recent trip. When you're on vacation, you're generally open to meeting new people, having fun, and experiencing new things—without worry or anxiety about where it will lead or how you will feel tomorrow. This is the spirit I encourage you to embrace when you meet someone new.

8

Risk = Reward

Our lives improve only when we take chances—and the first and most difficult risk we can take is to be honest with ourselves.

—Walter Anderson

I admire failures. I mentioned this to someone, and he responded, "Funny—I try to be inspired by people who have found success. Call me crazy!" I understand his logic, of course, but show me one highly successful person who has never failed at anything. There is probably more to learn from the roadblocks encountered on the path to success than from every moment of glory.

When failure is the result of a chosen course of action, it's usually because a certain amount of risk was undertaken. It's much harder to mess up if you are satisfied with the status quo and refuse to rock the boat.

Risk taking is one of my values. The greatest moments in my life have resulted from pushing past my comfort zone and exploring something unknown—whether it was a new experience, country, or relationship.

When I finished grad school in Toronto and moved to California without a job or a work visa, it was not a practical move. (Dear INS: If you are reading this, I did get legal status to work in the United States within my first few months of residing here) When I was boarding the plane with all my baggage (literally . . . and, well, figuratively), I was aware that heading to San Francisco was probably not the most sensible action, but I realized that I did not want to live my life with regret because I was scared to take a risk. I followed my heart across the continent to the West Coast to spend more time with a man that I subsequently lived with for 5 years. At the time, though, I had no idea what would happen, and I certainly didn't want to rely on him, or any one person, to build my new life. I knew that when I arrived in California, I would have to seek out friendships and find an employer to sponsor me as a foreigner. The truth is, when we follow our wants in life and take the necessary risks to achieve them, most of us discover that we are more resourceful than we gave ourselves credit for.

Risk taking is the ultimate rebellion against the shoulds of your life. It is directly related to fulfilling your dreams and living an authentic life.

A very wise and wealthy businessman once said to me (in his deep Charlton Heston voice), "Andrea, don't you know that you have to risk happiness to find happiness?" I walked away wondering what he meant. Do we have to struggle to be happy? I certainly hope not. And then it hit me—we can keep doing the same things we always do, lead a pleasant enough life, and be truly content. But happiness and contentment are not synonymous. To be happy is to access another level of engagement. In this way, happiness is about action. You realize that to *enjoy* your life, you have to create it. You realize that great things don't just happen— they have to be dreamed up, believed in, and built.

Repeat after Me . . .

It takes a lot of courage to step outside of your comfort zone. Your gremlins are often the most active when you break from your usual pattern. Here's the mantra I like to use when I take a risk: "I'm scared *and* I'll do it anyway!"

When I talk about taking risks in love, I'm not referring to going home with a stranger you meet at a bar, nor am I suggesting you start dating married men. I'm not talking about reckless behavior—actions that provide immediate gratification but later become a source of regret (and a few hard-earned lessons). I'm talking about the risks that you may be reluctant to take because they are not the easiest choices but that later become turning points in your life. These kinds of risks require you to put yourself out there in a bold and unpredictable way because you are guided by your gut and led by your feelings.

I remember being in a past relationship and wishing I could look into a crystal ball to find out whether I should stay or leave. I wanted a sign—something to indicate the next step I should take. But life, unfortunately, does not work that way. We are not given the answer before we take action. Risk taking is necessary to create change in our lives.

The funny thing is, while playing it safe is almost always the easier option, it rarely feels good. Most of the time, sitting on the fence feels stagnant and less comfortable than jumping off and landing on one side. Certainly the fall may hurt, but don't fool yourself—the fence rail digging into your thighs as you sit there hurts more.

When I pursued a relationship with Michael, jumping off the fence meant following my heart despite the shoulds, the can'ts, and the uncertainty that awaited me on the other side. But it was in that unknown territory that I found my husband.

For many of the women whose real-life romances are featured in these pages, risk taking has been an integral part of their success. When Ruth met François, she took a risk by going on that camping trip. But she never doubted her instincts. "I wasn't husband hunting at the time," she explained. "It was an authentic choice. Once I accepted that my gut was telling me something, I never looked back."

As my friend Natalie said when she fell in love with her non-type, sometimes reconnecting with the right partner reconnects you with yourself.

Realizing Your Potential

A funny thing happened to me when I realized I was falling in love with a man who would never earn a six-figure income (unless teachers in this country start to receive better compensation!)—*I* worked harder than ever and found the career of my dreams. Early in our relationship, I remember thinking, "Okay, if Michael isn't able to be the breadwinner, why can't I be the breadwinner?" Imagine that! It might sound painstakingly obvious (and maybe even offensive to those of you who have always relied solely on your own income), but for me it was empowering to realize I could rely on myself, and my own abilities, to create the life I wanted.

In many ways, Michael's modest income was a catalyst for my professional development. The entrepreneur in me came out in full force. I scheduled meetings with investors and pitched creative business ideas that excited me (a self-described sleep junkie) to pop out of bed early every day, even after long nights spent researching. All of that effort didn't feel like work, because I was following my wants. As I gained clarity in love, I found clarity in other areas of my life, too. It's as if a portion of my brain—one that was previously full of chatter and confusion—was now open to other, more constructive pursuits.

I'm certainly not motivated solely by money. (If I were, I would have chosen a more lucrative path than writing or coaching!) The point is that I started to think bigger and to believe in my own potential when I was with a partner who truly "got" me and encouraged me to shoot for the stars. In doing so, I found a career that brings me great joy—one that I feel solidly connected to.

Many women now earn as much as or more than their male partners and don't need to rely on a man for financial stability. Women increasingly want to be with a partner who fulfills them on an emotional level and who supports their dreams and ambitions. One woman told me, "After seeing my mom struggle to find a job and pay bills after my father left, I realized I never wanted to be in that position. It's always been important to me to know that I can provide for myself."

I have also spoken with women who married high-powered men and found that their professional ambitions—which they had spent a lifetime building—took a backseat to their husbands' more lucrative careers. In these cases, there was an unequal balance of power within the relationships that eventually led to resentment.

My friend Rachel realized her potential when she entered a relationship with her "clean-cut and conservative" NT Colin. "Colin challenges me to think bigger, to chase my curiosities, to question things more," she said. "I never considered myself an intellectual, but he makes me feel like one. I never considered myself the marrying type, but I am because I am married to him. The truth is we were not each other's type. But now that we are together, I see that I have more in common with Colin than any man I've ever been with. He introduced me to his passions, and I did the same. In the end we both win."

Taking risks requires you to open your eyes and challenge longtime beliefs. Rachel learned that some of her past assessments about people—and herself—were wrong. "When you are open minded, you automatically create a bigger world to play in," she said. "The strange thing is that I was the one who was stereotyping people. Colin donates a lot of his money to charity, he plays piano, he loves Scrabble, he loves animals, he is fair and honest and kind—these are not traits that I thought I would find in a guy who has been in a college fraternity. Now I see how wrong I was. When you find the right man, you find another side of yourself."

Formula for Change

Change requires three things: consciousness (identifying how you feel and what you want), faith (believing you can get it), and action (committing to new steps to reach your goals).

Consciousness

Consciousness is being aware of your situation and paying attention to how you feel about it. Consciousness is about identifying what you want and looking at what you are doing to achieve it—or prevent yourself from achieving it. How are you getting in your own way in reaching what you want? I ask myself this every time I feel stuck and unsure about how to reach a goal.

Consciousness is also about perspective. How do you currently see your goal? Why is it important to you? How is your perspective affecting your success?

In Chapter 6, I introduced you to Debra, who made a conscious decision to break her dating pattern and find a man who would "paint his own fence." Debra met her husband the night after she made this internal shift and set this intention for her life. She admits that she might have overlooked him had she not brought consciousness to her dating pattern.

You start to see and do things differently when you articulate your wants and gain clarity on what you value most. Change happens when you consciously decide to confront your self-defeating patterns and commit to a new path.

Faith

Once you become conscious of what you want to attract into your life, you need to have faith that you can attain it. For some of you, this may mean leaving behind a framework of fear that has motivated you in the past. For example, if you are conscious of the fact that work is unsatisfying and aware that you want to embark on a new career path, it is essential that you have faith in yourself and your abilities before you attempt to change. Similarly, if you are afraid to put yourself out there, try new things, or take risks in love because you don't want to get hurt, you cannot hope to improve your love life. You have to believe—truly believe—that the cost-benefit ratio is in your favor when you take a risk. When I talk to women who are dating someone they like but who are afraid to explore a serious relationship, I ask them, "What is it costing you to date this person? What is it potentially costing you *not* to give him a chance?" You must have faith that if you stay open and take risks, you *will* attract the kind of partner you want.

The first time I meet with a new client or with a woman in one of my workshops, I ask, "What are some of your fears in dating?" After she records her fear, I ask her to write down a counterargument, based on faith, beside the fear. A few of my clients volunteered to share some of their fear-to-faith arguments:

- *Fear:* I want to get married, but to be really honest, I like my own space. I'm freaked out about sharing my bed with someone. I like having room and spreading out in my apartment.

  Counterargument: I also want a family—that's my biggest goal—and I will never get it if I can't share my home. I'll buy a king bed for me and my husband to sleep in with two separate duvet covers like I see in European hotels!

- *Fear:* Being open/vulnerable to someone.

  Counterargument: I can't have intimacy without vulnerability. I need to stay open if I want to attract true connection.

- *Fear:* I'll stay in a relationship that I don't want to be in, like I have done in the past. I'm scared of getting sucked in.

  Counterargument: I am smarter than that. I've learned from my past relationships and will catch myself if I repeat the pattern. I promise to trust myself and listen to my instincts this time.

- *Fear:* I'm scared that a guy won't like me after he gets to know me and my flaws, and I will end up alone again.

  Counterargument: If I don't take chances and start dating again, I am guaranteeing that I will end up alone.

Try this exercise yourself. On a piece of paper, write down some of your fears, and then challenge yourself to respond with faith. What do you learn about how you might be getting in your own way?

Action

Creating a new course of dating action starts with the conscious decision to take ownership of your previous choices; from there, you make a commitment to thinking and doing things differently. Stop focusing on what you do not have and start taking steps toward creating what you want! These steps may involve risk, but risk-based action inevitably creates change and gives you a better vantage point from which to make future decisions.

When you physically put yourself out there, expect to hear from your gremlins and to feel challenged. Going outside your comfort zone will cause some discomfort and adjustment. When you try a new high-intensity gym class or work out with a heavier set of weights, your muscles will feel sore the next day, but that's how you know that your routine is working and that you are getting stronger. If you take risks in dating and you face rejection or you do not hit it off with the first man you meet, don't use that experience to justify quitting. You won't always succeed—but that doesn't mean you're not on the right path.

The key point to remember is that by applying consciousness, faith, and action, you are doing everything in your power to improve your situation. There are many things in this world that we can't control; isn't it worth taking action where we can?

Finding a Pearl

Risk taking lends itself to the use of metaphors, and Chinese proverbs on the subject abound. I have two favorites: "Pearls lie not on the seashore. If thou desirest one, thou must dive for it." And "Whether or not a dumpling is decently filled with meat cannot be judged from how well the decorative folds are made on the outside."

Sometimes you have to risk dating someone outside your comfort zone—someone who excites you. When you decide to follow your gut, you may discover that, as the proverb says, a pearl lies within your oyster. (Or, like the proverbial dumpling, he is more delicious than you could have imagined.)

I have my own metaphor for the risk of dating an NT. Think of your dating pool as a pile of presents waiting to be unwrapped. The NT may not be the shiniest or most neatly wrapped present in the pile, so it may not be the first one you reach for. You may place your bets, instead, on the dazzling box in the middle—until you open it and realize that the best part of that present was the packaging. Inside the box may be a generic item that has little value to you. Or the box may contain one of those Russian nesting dolls that you keep opening and opening until you are left with one teensy-weensy (though cute) doll. Trust me—the novelty of that doll wears off quickly.

When you reach for the simply wrapped box, you might open it without much thought, care, or expectation. But as you open it, you may be delighted to discover that what is inside becomes—like many NTs—the most perfect gift for you.

SMART Goals

Taking risks is a brave and necessary step on your way to creating change. Fortunately, a system of planning and preparation can make you more likely to reach your goals.

You may have heard about SMART goals. Some businesses in the United States train employees in this goal-setting system. SMART is an acronym; in the life-coaching community, SMART goals are defined as specific, measurable, action oriented (and I add "with accountability"), realistic, and with a time line. SMART goals create a structure for measuring your progress so that you feel your goals are attainable.

When you follow each SMART step, you are more likely to find success—whether you're trying to find your mate, get a new job, or lose 10 pounds. In contrast, if you create a list of dozens of goals that are not specific or manageable, you set yourself up for a challenging path and will feel frustrated when you fall short of your expectations. It's like dieters who set out to lose a bunch of weight right away and then give up when the scale doesn't budge after a week of dieting. "Why not eat those chips?" they think. "It doesn't matter anyway."

If your goal is to get married by Christmas and you are single in September, you're probably not positioning yourself for success, and you may actually sabotage your big-picture goal of settling down. By using the SMART goal framework, you define the microsteps needed to reach your ultimate goal. Here's how it works.

Specific

Define exactly what you want. Rather than skipping ahead several steps to "I want to get married by Christmas" or writing down something as general as "I want a boyfriend," focus on specific actions you can take *now* to inch yourself closer to your goal. You could start with something like "I want to date more than usual this month."

Measurable

How will you know when you have reached your goal if you cannot measure your progress? Make your goal measurable by including details. For instance: "I will go on at least one or two dates a week this month and will say yes to men who are fun to talk to, even if they are not men I have considered dating in the past."

Action Oriented and with Accountability

What will you do to ensure you have at least one or two dates a week, and how will you know that you have followed through with your commitment? Be specific with your actions and follow-up plans. You may write, "I will try speed dating and sign up for some meetup groups in topics that interest me to ensure that I meet a large pool of singles who share similar interests. I will invite a girlfriend to join me, and we will be accountable to each other, or I will ask my sister to check in with me to make sure I attended some of these events."

Realistic

Set yourself up for success by aiming for a goal within reach. Always review your goal and make sure you schedule the time to reach it. This may mean that you have to say no to something else in your life to clear room for this important goal. For example, you may write, "Finding a boyfriend is my most important goal this year. For this reason, I will say no to staying at work past 7:00 p.m. this month so that I have more time for dating. I may have to arrive at work earlier to make sure this is possible."

Time Line

Life coaches love to ask "By when?" each time a client defines a goal. As TV advice guru Dr. Phil says, "The difference between a dream and a goal is a time line!" Take out your calendar and target dates that will be your deadlines for each step. Tell a friend or set an alarm on your phone to remind you.

Some examples of dates in your calendar may include the next speed dating or Meetup.com event you will attend or the deadline you set for joining a new online dating site.

Take into account that great love and great achievements involve great risk.

—The 14th Dalai Lama

Change Is Here

By taking risks, you step into the change you want to create and honor your beliefs about who you are and what you want. Disable the snooze button on your life! It's time to get out of your comfort zone and wake up to new possibilities. It is time to jump off that fence and *create* them . . . even if you land on the wrong side of the fence a few times along the way.

Exercises

1. Imagine it's your 20-year anniversary with your partner, and friends have thrown you and your husband a party. What would your anniversary speech convey to your husband and friends?

2. Write down your goals. For each goal, write down three steps that require action. For example, your goal might be to go out on a blind date. What would you do to reach that goal?

Goal: **Blind Date**	
Action:	
1.	E-mail friends to ask if they know anyone to set you up with.
2.	Research a place you'd be comfortable meeting a stranger.
3.	Organize your calendar so that you have a few free nights available.

3. Taking risks is about more than physical action (such as flying across the country to give love a shot). It's also about taking emotional strides. What emotional and physical risks are you willing to take this week?

4. Think of one of your greatest achievements. Was it easy to reach? Was it the safest option available?

9

In Love with an NT: Dealing with Others Who Just Don't Get It

After you recover from the initial shock of falling in love with that guy who just wasn't your type, it is such a thrill to know that you've finally found your partner. In my case, I realized Michael was for me when I couldn't wait to share my life with him and found myself looking forward to picking wedding venues. (Remember, my nickname for years was Runaway Bride, and my love label was "commitment-phobe.") It's liberating to gain clarity on the kind of person who makes a good partner for you and to throw out old dating checklists and labels in favor of a deeper, more soulful, more fulfilling connection.

Of course, love fills our brains with endorphins. When you first pair up with your NT, you will be on a high; for better or for worse, no matter how great the hurdle, you love your NT and want to be with him.

When Michael and I realized we were falling in love, everything seemed to taste better. We visited a local ice-cream shop and were convinced that the ice cream we shared was the best we had ever tasted. (We now know the ice cream there is positively mediocre.) I had a "falling in love" glow (many people told me I looked better than usual), and I was suddenly a superhuman who required no more than 3 or 4 hours of sleep a night.

Science backs these symptoms of punch-drunk love. Dr. Helen Fisher, a biological anthropologist who has studied the effects of love on the human body, found that when people describe themselves as "head over heels in love," the pleasure centers in their brains light up with activity. In particular, two brain chemicals (dopamine and norepinephrine) are secreted in greater amounts. These chemicals are associated with feelings of happiness, elation, greater focus, and goal-directed behavior.[*]

When you realize you have fallen in love with your NT and embrace your connection, those pleasure centers in your brain have a tendency to override all other functions. You may find yourself thinking, "Who cares if he doesn't look like Prince Charming? It doesn't matter that he's a little introverted! So what if he and I are from different countries and cultural backgrounds? All that matters is that we're in love!"

That last thought—the one in which you silently (or even loudly) celebrate your happiness and newfound love—is like one of those happy movie scenes that's accompanied by epic music . . . right before the record needle is suddenly yanked away with an ear-piercing *scre-e-e-e-ech!*

---

[*] Richard Nicastro, "Relationship Help: How the Latest Research Can Transform Your Relationship" (April 13, 2008), retrieved from http://www.articlesbase.com/marriage-articles/relationship-help-how-the-latest-research-can-transform-your-relationship-385866.html.

Family Matters

It turns out that some people will have an issue with your relationship. Family members and friends may not be thrilled initially with the fact that you have chosen an NT. You can't blame them. You probably would have thought the same thing before you opened yourself to this NT relationship. And while your loved ones usually want the best for you, it may take them a while to realize that your NT is just that.

My friend Lahna's parents pleaded with her not to date her overweight comedian boyfriend, Ralphie. "My mom was so eager to get me out of the relationship with Ralphie and into a relationship with a nice Jewish doctor that she tried to set me up with her gynecologist!" Lahna recalled.

It was too late for a setup, though. Lahna was in love with Ralphie and had to come to terms with the fact that her family, and many outsiders, would judge their relationship.

"There were so many ways my parents challenged me when I started to date Ralphie," Lahna said. "Sometimes it was about me and my poor judgment. Other times, it was an attack on him. My reaction was always a fragile one. When you love people in your life who say things that are hurtful, it is usually not the first time they have done it. You've heard some of the complaints or judgments before, and it brings up other stuff. Anyway, who is ever prepared to put up with criticism from loved ones? Most of us want their support."

How did Lahna deal with the criticism from her family? She built emotional and mental walls to protect her when they launched into attacks against her relationship. The hardest part was her parents' embarrassment about her boyfriend, but Lahna felt that their reaction was driven by the fear of how their own peers would react.

Be Ready

Come up with a sound bite you can use in response to challenges to your relationship. For instance: "Thanks for your concern. I'm really happy. I promise to reach out if I need your advice, as I value it."

Lahna tried to consider her parents' perspective. "If my kids grow up and one is gay or different from how I expect them to be, I want my children to know that I support their choices and they should live their own lives," she said. "But for other parents, it's heartbreaking when the people they raised make life decisions that they don't understand. Even though my mom said mean things about Ralphie, I know she was operating from a place of love and protection. I often had to remind myself of that fact, even if I didn't agree with her words."

Now, with two beautiful grandchildren to adore and almost a decade's worth of evidence that Ralphie makes their daughter happy, Lahna's parents are more accepting of her relationship than she ever thought they'd be. Lahna admitted that it still occasionally hurts her feelings when others judge her relationship, but she could not ask for a better partner. Society is evolving to catch up with some of our less-conventional choices, she added. "It used to be illegal for a white person to be with someone black. Imagine how crazy it would be not to love someone because everyone else says it's wrong. Why do some of us still do that?"

A few years after we graduated, my college roommate, Monika, found love with a man (her CNT!) who has a young son. She had never pictured herself dating a man with a child, so she did not even consider dating Dave when they first met at work.

Once Monika realized she was in love with Dave for the long term, she decided to keep silent about her boyfriend's fatherhood when she introduced him to her mom and dad. Monika's father, a traditional Catholic from Poland, did not believe in divorce, let alone raising a child as a single parent. Dave did not understand why she would hide his son from her family, but she knew how to anticipate her parents' reaction. Her strategy was to give her very traditional parents the opportunity to get to know (and hopefully like) Dave before they judged him for being a single father.

Monika remembered, "I was trying to hide his circumstance so they could give him a fair shot. I knew they would not understand his situation because their frame of reference is so different. I was very open with Dave about my family and explained to him that they came from a different perspective—one that is informed by a different religion and culture—and divorce is very foreign to them. In a way, I didn't blame my parents for this. I knew they were rooted in their previous culture, and trying to transfer that to a different context is difficult for them."

Dave understood the situation but did not have a lot of patience for it. "Dave found this odd," Monika remembered, "but I wanted him to be accepted by my family and explained that he had to trust me when it came to my own family and the way things are done. I reiterated to Dave that it wasn't me and that I wasn't embarrassed by him or his circumstances, but that I wanted to make a positive start."

When you introduce your NT to friends and loved ones, you don't want to sabotage the chances that he'll be viewed objectively instead of simply being assigned a label. In Monika's case, she knew that her parents would have labeled Dave "single dad" and nothing more. If you feel that gradually introducing your NT to loved ones gives him the best chance of winning them over, talk to him about your approach and make sure he is comfortable with this strategy.

At some point, though, the dreaded elephant must be invited into the room. I asked Monika how she finally told her parents that Dave was a father. "I did it in phases," she admitted. "First, I introduced Dave as my boyfriend and let them get to know each other. Then, many months later, after I knew my mother really liked him, I told her the whole story. I explained that Dave and his ex-girlfriend were surprised by an unplanned pregnancy, that he tried to make it work with her, and that he was a very committed father to his little boy. My mom was more open minded than I thought she would be, and I'm sure it's because she had gotten to know Dave over the months."

Monika waited even longer to talk to her even more old-fashioned and hot-tempered father. Monika told me that while she, her sister, and her mother were stalling for time and trying to figure out the best way to tell her dad, in the end, the news slipped out of Dave's mouth. "It's hilarious when you think about it," Monika laughed as she remembered. "My dad and Dave were talking about how much Dave loved living in Australia, and my dad asked him why he left the country. Without thinking, Dave responded, 'I left Australia because of my son.' To which my dad replied, 'Oh. Too much sun?'" Dave explained that no, that's not what he meant—and confessed what everyone else had been hiding for him. After a long, silent, nervous pause in which everyone held their breath, Monika's father looked up and said, "Do you have any photos of your son?"

Monika said the wacky approach worked because her dad was already invested in a relationship with Dave. He already liked and respected him. "So when Dave told my dad what happened and about how he was committed to his son, my father felt like he knew Dave enough to know Dave was an upstanding person." She added,

"I know for a fact that if my dad had not had a relationship with Dave, there is no way he would have accepted it. It would have taken him years to give Dave a chance."

When you give your NT mate and your loved ones a chance to bond before providing full disclosure about your situation, you may be surprised to find that they take his unexpected NT qualities in stride. Chances are, they'll be more open to him than you may have initially anticipated when you thought about how much your folks would "kill you" for bringing "someone like that" home.

We can't necessarily fault our loved ones for assessing our mate from their own perspective. When you were born, your parents probably imagined the kind of life they wanted for you, which may have looked much different from the life you've chosen for yourself. You don't have to agree with their reaction—but do try to be patient as they get used to your unconventional or, in their eyes, "risky" choice. They may need time to understand and accept your situation.

If it seems like they're not ever going to come around, don't get defensive too fast. Consider that your family and friends know you well and are looking out for your long-term interests, which can often be harder for you to see clearly when you are in love. In some cases, they may see something that you don't. Be open to their comments. Learn to differentiate between constructive criticism and superficial criticism of your partner.

In extreme cases, families disown or cut off communication with loved ones who make romantic choices they do not support. By no means do I wish to underestimate the gravity of these situations. If you find yourself in a predicament in which your parents threaten to pull away permanently, you will have to weigh what you are willing to lose in exchange for your partner.

Family therapy with a trained professional can be helpful in these situations.

Feeling Confident about Your Decision

My friend Natalie found true love with Dale, someone who was completely different from her "perfect" former husband. She rarely concerns herself with how other people view her relationship. "When I introduced my ex-husband to people, I used to ask, 'So—what do you think?' " she admitted. "I never ask that question anymore. I know Dale is it for me, and it doesn't matter what anyone thinks. I don't need to get approval. It's quite refreshing, actually!"

I asked Natalie if her parents were concerned that Dale's job might eventually take them to another state or even out of the country. Natalie responded that while she knows her mother would object to such a move, she has made her peace with the possibility. "I think that when you're in the right relationship, you do things for yourself a little more," she said. "When you're not, you stay in relationships that may not work in order to satisfy others."

Ruth knew that getting her conservative Jewish parents to approve of her relationship with her younger, French-Canadian, Catholic boyfriend might be tough. But she knew the relationship was worth fighting for.

"It never crossed my mind to end it with François," she explained. "I love my parents, and having them accept my partner was and is important; but I remember thinking that if they didn't approve, it wouldn't stop me. I did not look back."

Naturally, her parents may have preferred François to come in an Anglo-Jewish package, but they have adjusted well. "Once they got to know François and saw how we were together, it helped them understand our relationship," Ruth said.

Peer Pressure?

When you pursue a nontype, you have to be ready to face not just the pressures of your family but also the reactions of your friends. If they really are your friends, of course, they want you to be happy. But they may also be protective of you, and your choice may challenge their expectations of the right person for you. They may be uncomfortable seeing a different side of you, or they may think you can "do better."

These reactions are a form of subtle peer pressure. Some of us experience this when we pair off with men who are not our usual type or the type others expect to see us with. We wish our friends could immediately see what we see in our mate, but we are prepared for the fact that they may not "get it" at first glance.

A creative-looking woman I recently met complained that her friends judge her older boyfriend, who she says is the best partner she's ever had. She threw her hands up in the air. "So the guy I'm with doesn't have tattoos and isn't 'cool.' And yes, he's a bit of a geek. So what? My friends keep telling me that they picture me with someone more like Lenny Kravitz. I don't even know what that means!" She was noticeably upset. I had to remind her not to take on other peoples' values as her own. Her friends aren't the ones whose lives will be most affected by her relationship choice.

She admitted, "I am happier with this guy than I expected to be. I love coming home to him, but I am still a little embarrassed to bring him to parties, since I know others won't understand."

I presented her with a practical question: Who would you

choose to marry—the man everybody likes when he walks through
the door at a party, or the man you really like when he opens the
front door at home?

For many women, it's hard to give up the idea that your partner should automatically click with your social circle. In Adriana's
case, she wondered how her NT would fit in with her friends, and
what everyone else in the room would think when she introduced
him. Most of Adriana's friends in New York date men who work in
finance, wear expensive clothes, and dine at pricey restaurants.
Her husband, Bill, is not like those guys, which is just fine with
Adriana. "I've questioned my friends and asked, 'Are you in love
with the guy or the life you can have with him?' Bill's values are
more important than his wallet, and I know I will have a stable life
with him."

It didn't take Adriana long to realize that no matter what the
people in her peer group thought, their opinions were less important than how she felt. "It's not their life—it's my life," she told me.
She advises other women in her situation to base their decisions
on whom they want to be with at the end of the day. In most cases,
people who are judgmental about your romantic choices reveal
much more about who they are and where their insecurities lie
than about you or your values.

Madeline admitted that she is occasionally self-conscious when
she attends gatherings with Tom's friends and everyone is older
than she is; she is still aware that when she brings Tom out with her
peers, some will judge their age difference. She told me that she
even prepares some friends who have not yet met Tom, since she
feels as if she has to give them advance warning.

But for every person who's questioned her choice, many more
have commented that she seems happier with Tom than she's
appeared to be in years. At one party, when Madeline sheepishly

pointed out her older boyfriend from across the room to an acquaintance, the woman responded, "Do you mean that fabulously sexy older man right there?" It just goes to show that sometimes we project values and reactions onto other people that are all wrong.

The truth is, aside from your closest friends, most of the people you socialize with—neighbors, co-workers, etc.—probably don't care who your boyfriend is. It's like how some women won't wear a bathing suit to the beach because they imagine everybody will stare or gawk, not realizing that most people are too focused on their own flaws to notice anyone else's. Unless you're wearing a bikini made of dental floss, you probably won't garner much attention!

When Anna started to date a single father, many of her loved ones warned her that her boyfriend wouldn't have enough time to devote to her because he had a daughter and a career. She took their concerns into account but ultimately decided to let Michael's actions speak for themselves. "I think it's important in dating anyone to go with your gut," Anna said. "If you can keep fear and insecurity out of it, then you should be able to heed your friends' and family's concerns but also do what feels right."

Many of Anna's friends still think she's made an unusual choice to be with a single dad—a choice they wouldn't make for themselves. That's okay with Anna, though. She is happy to have inherited "double the love." In fact, she wouldn't have it any other way.

Choosing What's Right for You

You can hear out, respect, consider, and understand the positions of the people in your life who have known you well and for a long time and who may be surprised by your choice of mate. But you don't have to agree with or honor their views by making life decision based on *their* needs and values.

Most of the women I've spoken with who married NTs faced some challenges with their families (except for the ones who left unkempt, directionless guys for DNTs who were clean-cut, driven ones—in those cases, their parents were thrilled!). But all of them said that once they gave their loved ones some time to adjust and a chance to get to know their mate, most relatives eventually came around.

Give your family an opportunity to express their concerns about your NT without interruption. Before you defend your relationship, acknowledge their position and reiterate that you have heard their points. You are more likely to be heard in turn if you establish an open and honest dialogue rather than enter the conversation with boxing gloves on. Remember, you can listen to their opinions *and* not follow their advice. You are an adult. If you live anybody's life but your own, you will wake up one day feeling unsatisfied and may not know why.

You are excited about your NT; you know he is a good person and partner for you. Allow your family and friends to express concerns, ask questions, catch up, and come around.

Stranger things have happened.

Exercises

1. When you're feeling challenged or misunderstood for your relationship choice, make a list of people who support you and whom you feel you can share with. Write down at least four people here that you know you can rely on:

   1. _____
   2. _____
   3. _____
   4. _____

2. We often feel stuck when we have an either/or decision thrust upon us. Look carefully. Is there a third option? What would it look like to respect your parents' intentions and feelings without letting them dictate your choices?

3. Imagine it's a year from now and this issue is fully resolved. What did you do to help create a positive outcome?

IO

The Ultimate Dating
Challenge

*Normally, we do not so much look at things as overlook
them.*

—*Alan Watts*

A few years ago, when I realized I was falling in love with Michael,
I told my 75-year-old Aunt Dorothy that I was worried he wasn't
perfect. My aunt simply said, "If you start from perfect, Andrea,
you have nowhere to go together." What a nice—and realistic—
perspective. After all, she should know. When she was a young
woman, she married a charming man with movie star looks (all
the gals liked him). She later ended up with my Uncle Al, a small-
town guy who owned the gas station she frequented. My Aunt
Dorothy and Uncle Al will be celebrating their 39th wedding
anniversary in September.

It's not as if all my concerns about Michael became irrelevant
when I realized that I loved him. Michael was less conventional
than my usual *type*. The fact that he wasn't polished and didn't
care about impressing strangers worried me. I am an extrovert; he

is an introvert. I attend networking events in my spare time; Michael would rather fiddle with his fish tank (does the water really need to be changed *that* often?) than engage in small talk with someone he will never see again. If it's important for me to have him there, he'll join me at these events—and can usually be found standing off to the side, on his own, observing the crowd. He encourages me to keep buzzing around the room and not to worry about whether he's enjoying himself. Michael and I have had to make compromises to meet halfway so that neither of us feels resentful and so that both our needs are met. Isn't that what partnership is about?

Unlike the men I dated before him, Michael doesn't always know what to say at a social function and couldn't care less about formality. People do not always see how charming he *really* is— not at first, anyway. In his own words, he is "an acquired taste"— he grows on people with time. Would I like it if Michael believed in wearing non-rubber-soled shoes and instantly impressed everybody he meets? Of course. But more than anyone I've ever met, he fulfills me on an emotional, physical, and spiritual level—and that, to me, is priceless.

We worry so much about what everybody will think when, in fact, we are the ones who have to go home with our mates and be with them in the quiet moments. Most of us need to ask ourselves if we like, respect, and feel excited about our partners when nobody else is there watching.

Every day of my marriage, I realize what a wonderful match I have found: someone who stretches me, inspires me, and helps keep my feet planted firmly on the ground even as he encourages me to go for the moon. I once thought that feeling comforted and being challenged were mutually exclusive, but now I know that feelings of stability and peace can coexist with sheer excitement and joy. I like who I am around my husband, and I feel he truly *sees* me. To me, that's the real essence and the true meaning of a soul mate.

My story, and the love stories of the women in the book who found happiness with their nontypes, is not unique. These scenarios happen everywhere, every day. Women accidentally fall in love with men they never pictured themselves marrying, and women surprise themselves when they realize they have feelings for a person whom they never thought they would see *that way*.

Somehow, though, many of us are still expecting—and even demanding—that our mates add up to our original vision of what we thought they would be. I cannot count how many single women have told me that they'll never "settle for less" than the husband they've always pictured marrying. Who could blame them? Advertisements, movies, TV shows, and dating guides advise women to find their Prince Charming. So many women I've spoken with are hoping to emulate what they see played out with "perfect" pairs in Hollywood. They are surprised when every other couple from the TV show *The Bachelor* does not work out. "They were so in love!" these women tell me. "They looked so good together and seemed so happy!" These same people find it unbelievable that sweet Sandra Bullock married Monster Truck daredevil Jesse James. They think it's weird that glamorous Courteney Cox settled down with quirky David Arquette.

I have met too many women who complain that their Mr. Right always seems to turn out to be, well, wrong. Why aren't we catching on?

Christine, my college friend who married a man a few inches shorter than herself (something that was once a deal breaker for her), asked me why women continue to evaluate men with the same criteria. "It certainly isn't a checklist that reflects all of their

> ## PMs Who *Are* Perfect for You
>
> Maybe the guy for you comes in the nicest packaging avail-
> able. Dating the nontype does not mean that you should
> disregard men who excite you *and* who happen to look really
> great on paper and in person. Power to you if you can find a
> man who has it all!

past successes, otherwise they would no longer require the list.
They'd be in a relationship with that perfect person. These lists
are based on the expectations of others, what they think they want
to feel to be whole, and on archetypal men created by Hollywood.
Those people don't exist!"

As we get older, our choices and values evolve. We date with more
discernment, considering how a man's qualities will translate over the
long term. You may still like a guy with light eyes and dark hair or
prefer someone who can own the dance floor at weddings, but eventually you realize that there are more important qualities to be had in
a long-term mate. Criteria that you used to identify with your type
may, at some point, no longer be relevant.

And it's not just superficial criteria, like good looks, that shift
over time. More substantial qualities that were must-haves in the
past can change based on what's happening in your life or in the
world around you. After the market crashed, one of my clients
edited her list from "The man I want to be with must have a good
job" to "The man I want to be with has to be driven and motivated." Even that small shift created different dating results that
more accurately reflect her values.

We have to make deeper choices. There is no reason for anyone
to have a midlife crisis in their 20s or 30s, terrified that they don't
yet have the life they've always hoped for. We must use new criteria

to measure our happiness in—and out of—a relationship. We must remember not to confuse immediate gratification with long-term fulfillment.

I believe that when you are with the right match you will know it is right not because of a thought, but a feeling . . . a feeling that you want to spend more time around him. It's a simple test, really: Do you want to be in a foxhole with him?

Who Is *Your* Best Self?

I am confident that I would not be my best self now if I'd married based on any other criteria than the reasons I chose to be with Michael. I was not my best self in past relationships, when I was completely confused and disconnected from my wants.

You know when you're not living up to your own potential with someone. And if you don't know, one good indicator is if the relationship seems to bring out your inner "crazy girl"—you constantly check your phone to see if he called, you stalk him on Facebook, or you consistently find yourself feeling defensive or insecure. How many times have you cried over the person you're dating? When you're in a relationship that is not balanced and happy, you may not even recognize yourself.

I dated some wonderful people in the past who were not wonderful partners for *me*. A good relationship is one in which you are seen—and celebrated—for who you are and one in which you are inspired to bring your partner to his best potential as well.

Let Go

Who doesn't love checking off boxes and crossing off items on a list? (In fact, sometimes I secretly make a list after I've completed a few tasks, just to cross them off.) We like to quantify our progress based on external achievements. It is more difficult to acknowledge how far we have traveled when the shift has happened internally.

Ruth, who married her French-Canadian NT, realized how far she had come when she recently bumped into a couple from her old apartment building who knew her as "the single lady who would die old with cats" (that was the label Ruth gave herself!). She used to admire this couple and think about how lucky they were to have found each other. When she saw them recently, they asked her about single life. Ruth, of course, mentioned that she was now married to François and had two children.

As she reflected on the conversation, she said, "Years ago when I saw this couple, I was envious of their relationship, and I thought about how much further along they were than I was . . . and now our children are the same age! Somehow we ended up being in the same spot. I never could have imagined that." Ruth admits that she had no idea how her life would unfold after her broken engagement and really believed she would end up as an old spinster who spent her time knitting sweaters (for her cats).

After finding great love with someone whom she never would have pictured being with, Ruth knows how important it is to take risks in romance. She told me that she has two words for people who are interested in a nontype but scared to date him: "*Let go!*"

Let go of your need to have the mate you think you *should* have, and embrace the one you *want* to be with. Let go of obsessing over the whos and the whens of your future. Let go of what anyone else will think. Stay present and let your life happen in real time.

"There is so much anxiety involved in finding the right partner," Ruth said. "Nowadays, women have so many choices. Just allow in whatever comes your way and be open to the possibilities of the unknown. When you choose a partner you really love, it transcends a lot of things, including everybody else's opinion. You'll see."

Ruth met François when she was doing a lot of improvisational comedy. Improv helped her tremendously in dating. It reminded her to be in the moment and make things up as she went along. Improv is also about saying yes and accepting the dialogue the other person on stage delivers to you—without trying to control the way the scene unfolds.

New Love Lists

Up until now, your dating pattern has not worked in your favor. Some of the criteria you used for your "type" may feel less significant now. I hope you will consider making new love lists and will commit to wearing a new love label. I hope you will challenge yourself by shaking up your current perspective.

I cannot emphasize enough that making a new checklist in love—or doing away with your checklist altogether—is *not* about giving up things that are important to you or running off with a guy whom you find unattractive and annoying. This is *not* what dating the nontype is about!

Rather, I encourage you to reassess and refocus your priorities—to make a new checklist that is based on your values and other essential criteria. You aren't giving up anything—you are gaining the insight and the ingredients that are more likely to work over the long haul.

The ultimate dating challenge is to challenge *yourself.* Your dating success starts with you.

As my colleague Lisa says, "Want a different dating result? Do something different consistently. Be different. Pay attention differently. Attract differently. And be open to a different result."

Once you confront your dating pattern and remove the negative love label you've been wearing, take that step outside your comfort zone. Call back those guys who intrigued you but who you ruled out because they didn't "seem right"; book a date with a man who is shorter, balder, grayer, or heavier than you; or answer an e-mail from the guy whom you were curious about but who "lives too far away." Take a risk. Stay open. Log on to a few dating sites and play with the parameters for height, age, income, and distance. See who shows up. If you usually date men who like to be the center of attention, try dating someone quieter who gives you the stage. See how *you* show up. The ultimate dating challenge is not really about landing a certain kind of person—it is about becoming the person you are meant to be.

New Love Labels

When I used to think about getting married, I worried that a part of me would forever be lost. (Seriously—who thought of the horrible term *settling down*?!) My biggest dating fear was that I would shrink when I had to share my life and commit to someone long term. I held on to my label of commitment-phobe with a strange sense of pride. I somehow found it comforting to exist in intimate relationships with one foot out the door. I could maintain a false sense of control over my love life and not expose my heart too much. In doing so, I may have protected myself from getting hurt, but I also cut myself off from intimacy.

I do feel *settled* in my relationship, and with that feeling my perspective has changed. Now I see that with the right match, you don't have to give up your identity. You can be who you are *and more*. Whereas I believed I would shrink with a partner, in fact I feel that I have expanded. I feel safer now that I've allowed a healthy relationship into my life.

My friend Lahna, who married her comedian friend Ralphie when he did not have a lot of money and was at his heaviest weight, never offers excuses for following her instinct to be with him. Making the decision to be with Ralphie was empowering because it was an authentic choice. "You have to live your own life," she said. "I wasn't planning on marrying Ralphie when I met him. I'm with him because of who he is and how he made me feel. Find your best friend, find a good partner. Now Ralphie and I have two little people we're both responsible for. It's a lot of work, so you'd better love the person you're doing the work with."

My wish for you is that you give yourself permission to pursue a romantic relationship with someone who may not add up on paper, but who treats you well and truly gets who you are. I hope you will focus less on how this person looks to outsiders and consider how he makes you feel on the inside.

When Your Nontype Becomes Your Type

My friend Natalie left her marriage to a "perfect," well-mannered guy and ended up with Dale, a man she describes as a midwestern rebel. She realizes now that her current partner's qualities are more suited to her and her lifestyle than those of the men she used to pursue. Before dating Dale, she pictured pairing off with a sensitive, new-agey guy—the kind of men who surrounded her in her native California. The funny thing is, Natalie admitted, "Dale was probably *always* my type. I just didn't know it. He has all the qualities that are most important to me."

Perhaps your true type is the one whom you have never dated or have not yet considered as a realistic option (even when you have been drawn to people like him). Cynthia, my friend and fellow coach who married her NT, put out a great dating challenge.

She said, "What if we just let go of all our must-haves and trusted that we would attract the person perfect for us? What do we all want? To be loved, respected, adored. I think the list is pretty simple, really. We complicate it with all of our expectations."

Is it possible that we overcomplicate and overthink our love lives? Could the cliché "When you're with the right match, you know" actually be true?

I believe that sometimes we do *know*—in our gut or in our heart—when things are right or wrong with a man, but many times we are afraid to admit it. Sometimes we know our personal truth and are fully aware of what we want, but we don't know what will happen if we say it out loud. We are worried that if we express what we *really* want, others may hold us to it . . . or worse yet, we may hold ourselves to it. Sometimes when we declare a want, we worry that we are setting ourselves up for disappointment if we can't find it—so we trick ourselves into believing we don't really want it. The reality is that being authentic is the easiest thing you can be. You have to speak your truth, or it will find you.

Throughout your dating life, your gut may gently tap on your brain, asking it to make a decision, or may scream at your heart to "Let go!" or "Let him in!" As a woman, you have the gift of tremendous sensitivity and intuition, so use it to your advantage. Harnessing your intuition entails drowning out many of the shoulds you've absorbed from your family and other sources (remember, those are *their* shoulds and values) and confronting the negative self-talk and labels you may be holding on to.

Here's the good news (see—I told you I'm an optimist): Doing this is easier than you may realize. Once you start honoring your wants, you may not understand how you ever ignored your instincts. Clarity rushes in and spills all over everything in your life when you live consciously and authentically, and navigating life feels much easier. Usually when you taste that kind of clarity, you cannot go back to lying to yourself.

In my case, once I let go and allowed my heart to admit to my head that Michael was the right partner for me, my life became a lot less confusing. My "clarity" e-mail password seems funny to me now, but it reminds me how important it is to live with clarity and consciousness every day. (Though now that I've publicized my e-mail password to the world, I will change it . . . to some new theme I want to attract into my life!)

Live Authentically

Focus on yourself and being the most authentic you can be. When you are living authentically, you are more likely to attract an authentic match. When you are feeling aligned and connected to your wants, you have a better vantage point from which to make decisions.

Don't live anybody's truth but your own. It is simply exhausting and absolutely unfulfilling to embody other peoples' values. You have one life—so stand firm and proud in it!

Don't date a nontype to spite anyone. Date a nontype in spite of anyone's opinion if your NT makes you happy and if you feel more clarity, peace, and joy than you have experienced with a partner before. Look around at your friends, family, and community. I bet you will find many women who can tell you about their happy relationships with men they never expected to love. In fact, let's ditch the Prince Charming fairytales and start telling *those* stories.

There are no rules for your happiness in a relationship other than this: Don't settle for anyone who does not help you be the best version of you and who isn't someone you want to be with in the quiet moments . . . because if you do marry Perfect Man but you are not enjoying your life or living at your best potential with him, I can assure you that all his pretty packaging won't really matter.

Surprise yourself. Surprise others. Date men you would date if nobody was looking.

Exercise

We've all heard the expression "Never say never." When has it applied in your life?

FILL IN THE BLANKS:

I am _____

I want _____

I know that _____

_____

HERE ARE A FEW THINGS I'VE LEARNED ABOUT MYSELF RECENTLY:

_____

_____

_____

Appendix

Dating Tips to Find Your NT

Online Dating:
Dos and Don'ts

Online dating is a great way to challenge yourself to date people you may not otherwise have a chance to meet in life. It is also an excellent opportunity to get out there and stretch and strengthen your dating muscles.

Recently, I answered a phone call from a friend who had recently returned home from a date with a man she met online. Without uttering so much as a polite "hello," she barked, "He looked *nothing* like his photo and was about a decade older!"

Sound familiar?

The number one complaint voiced by online daters is that the person they meet is different from the person they saw online.

Writing an online dating profile is like writing a good cover letter when you apply for a job—its sole purpose is to capture the reader's interest so that he wants to meet you and learn more. And here's the good news: You *can* market yourself effectively without inventing a whole new persona.

Online daters come across many profiles. How do you help yours stand out from the crowd? Believe it or not, simple steps like checking your spelling, posting a good photo, and keeping the information concise and upbeat can be the difference between someone following up with you or clicking on someone else's profile.

Here are the essential Dos and Don'ts for constructing your online dating profile.

Do Post Photos

Most people miss the boat if they don't attach at least one photo to their profiles. If you're too shy to include a picture upfront, make it clear that you will offer a photo if you feel a connection with someone who writes to you. Just be aware, however, that many—if not most—online daters won't even consider a profile if it lacks a photo.

Don't Post Many Photos

I know—you have many cute looks: career woman on-the-go, down-home girl posed with her family, or sexy vacation companion with that really great tan from Mexico. Even so, resist the urge to post more than a couple of photos. Otherwise you'll overwhelm your audience, who won't have a clue which photo best captures you today. The rule is to post a couple of photos—ideally one close-up and one full-body shot.

Do Post a Photo of Yourself *Solo*

Your niece may be really adorable, or you may want to show that you hang out with cute members of the opposite sex, but it's better to stay solo in your photo online. And on that note, don't include a photo where you've cut off someone's arm wrapped around you. C'mon! Digital cameras make it easy to get at least one good shot of you on your own!

Do Create a Compelling Essay

Do be concise and specific to capture the reader's interest. Instead of saying "I love to travel," mention the best trip you've ever taken. Replace "I have a good sense of humor" with something witty. Bottom line: Show, don't tell!

Do have someone else (preferably of the opposite sex) proof your profile to make sure it flows, highlights your best qualities, and is free of spelling and grammatical errors.

Remember, online dating is like speed dating—you have a small window to make a big impression.

Don't Be Too Cool for Online Dating

If you've made the decision to date online, don't feel you have to apologize or be embarrassed—you will only insult the potential matches who have made the same choice. Don't justify why you're dating online or make statements like "My mother made me do this, but I hate online dating." Stay upbeat and humorous without being jaded or condescending.

Do Be Honest

Finally, a note about honesty: Lying about your relationship status, the way you currently look, or exaggerating certain characteristics are cardinal online dating sins.

One of my friends insists that the majority of men who post their height as 5 foot 9 are 5 foot 7 or under. Many women who post as 29 years old are actually over 30. It's not good to embellish, since a big part of dating is about clear expectations. And really, do you want to start out a relationship by being dishonest?

Online dating can be like a big bargain sale—you may have to sift through junk to find the gems. Don't let that deter you! There are some amazing singles, more than 40 million of them (that's almost half the single population!), who are also looking online for love and hoping to meet you, too.

First Dates:
Getting Past the Jitters

You're about to go on a date with someone you really like. You've been dreaming about it and dreading it at the same time. You feel like a fraud. That photo your date has seen of you shows you at your best. Your hair never looks that good! You're rarely as cool or charming as you appeared when you booked the get-together. Your date will notice all this, and the whole evening will be uncomfortable. Now you're thinking about canceling the date, because it's not worth the potential embarrassment.

STOP!

Self-doubt and nerves can get the best of us on any date, but there's no reason to let first-date jitters ruin what could be a lot of fun.

Keep these tips in mind to manage your nerves and ace the first date.

Be Curious

A frequent complaint both men and women have after a first date is that the other person talked too much and didn't ask questions or listen.

People notice when you notice them. There's no need to

conduct 20 questions—a few specific questions about your date's interests is a good place to start. Share some things about yourself, too, so the date becomes a conversation and not a job interview.

When you focus your attention on the other person and worry less about what you're going to say next, you're more likely to relax and stay in the moment—which will lead to a more successful date.

Do an Activity Together

Shake up the usual dinner-and-drinks routine and suggest going for a walk, playing pool, bowling, dancing, ice skating, or engaging in another public activity on your date. It'll be easier to communicate when you have something else to focus on—and doing something active and fun will probably lead to a better date, anyway!

Find Common Ground

What brought you together in the first place? Did you pick each other up? Did you meet through friends? Whatever brought you together is an obvious jumping-off point for conversation.

Hint: There's no need to e-stalk, but if you want to feel extra-prepared or find something in common before you meet up, type your date's name into a search engine and see if you can glean something about his background. (Just make sure not to tell your date that you read the 88 posts about him or cite specific details of his fellowship in Ecuador 14 years ago!)

Highlight Your Passions

People light up when they talk about things that they care deeply about. Show your exciting and passionate side and you will show your date that you are charismatic and confident, which are two of the most attractive qualities you can possess.

If you don't know what you're passionate about, think of one of your favorite memories. Were you running a marathon, hanging out with family, relaxing up at the cottage? Use one as a conversation starter.

Remember—It's Just a Date!

When you're feeling first-date jitters, remember that the person you're going out with was attracted enough to book the date with you in the first place!

Don't approach a first date with the expectation that it has to mean XYZ. Don't plan what you're going to say next when your date is talking or second-guess everything that comes out of your mouth. Stay present and have fun.

You may psych yourself up only to realize the person you're out with isn't a match for *you*. That's okay. A date is simply an opportunity to spend time with someone new and see if there's potential for more. Remember: A first date is all about possibility—not pressure.

10 Steps to Dating Success

1. Try to identify some of your fears in a relationship.

Look at how these influenced your last relationship. Are you prepared to take steps to face your fears? If your fear was losing your independence, how will you act in your next relationship to ensure you don't get lost in a partnership? If your fear is that nobody else will accept your silly habits, look at these habits closely and determine if they're really so terrible. Most important, make some new relationship resolutions to try to reframe some of your fears.

2. Write out what you know to be true about the amazing things you bring to a relationship. Don't be modest!

Why would somebody be lucky to be with you? What makes you unique? How are you a loving partner when you feel good in a relationship? What kinds of wonderful things do you do for friends and loved ones? If you're struggling with this step, enlist friends to help you answer these questions.

3. If you are processing a recent breakup, ask yourself—why did you stay as long as you did?

Were there moments when you knew the relationship wasn't working? How did you deal with those issues? What would you do differently if you did it again? What have you learned for next time? (I always tell clients not to replay fights in their minds and wish that the outcome had been different. Very rarely is a fight about the thing you're fighting about!)

4. Allow yourself time to grieve in whatever way feels comfortable to you *today*.

For some women, playing sad love songs and spending a night or two inside with Ben and Jerry are ideal ways to cope. For others, jumping into the dating game and kissing a few new guys serves as the best distraction.

(*Note*: Don't allow people to tell you what you *should* feel or do.)

5. If you feel ready to start meeting and kissing new guys, put out the feelers. Network to create your own possibilities.

Various studies show that the majority of singles meet their future spouse through their family, friends, or social network. When you're looking for a job or a new place to live, you network to find opportunities. Approach dating the same way! It's all about attitude—if you act like you're ready to have fun and would love to meet someone great, people will be compelled to help. Ask *five* people if they know anyone you may be interested in meeting. Once you've completed the must-have/can't stand exercise in Chapter 3, you can select a few things from your list to illustrate the kind of person you're looking for.

Here's a tip: Enlist the help of people you don't know well—perhaps someone from work or a friend of a friend you like. Chances are they have access to people who aren't already in your network.

6. Sign up for 1 to 3 months of online dating.

Get over any objections that online dating isn't a romantic way to meet somebody or that it's not "you" to post an ad. Think about it: Chances are you know somebody—or have a connection to somebody—who met a partner online. You may sift through some less-than-perfect matches in the process, but think of the funny stories and dating practice you'll gain. (Remember: Even a bad date makes a great story!) More important, there's a good chance you'll make a connection—or at least expand your network, which may lead to a connection with someone else.

7. Talk to strangers and always smile.

I'm not suggesting you tap the shoulder of every person who walks by, but challenge your comfort zone. Ask the guy slicing your deli meat how his day has been or what he loves about his job; ask the secretary at your dentist's office how many people she hears scream from her chair. Get comfortable making conversation so that when you lock into somebody you'd really like to chat with, you can approach it with the same amount of confidence, curiosity, and warmth.

8. Be curious and open—even if you have to fake it.

Men want approval. They don't want to feel that a woman is going to change, judge, or criticize them. This is *not* to say that a man doesn't want to be challenged. Just as there's a difference between a conceited guy and a confident one, there's a difference between being a critical woman and a challenging one.

The way to intrigue and challenge a guy is to ask open-ended and specific questions—be curious! Instead of asking him what his job is, ask him something like "What's your favorite part of a weekend?" or "How is living in New York different from your experience in California?" These questions will likely surprise and engage him. If they don't—he's probably not open or interesting enough for you!

9. "Pick up" single women.

I'm not advocating that single women try bisexuality (but if you'd like to, go for it!). By picking up single women, I mean meeting new women at parties, book clubs, the gym, or other social outings so that you're more likely to enjoy your singlehood.

One issue that single women often face is that they feel as though the majority of their friends have significant others. It's nice to go to your friend and her husband's home for dinner (even when their baby is eating Cheerios at the table), but it's also nice to go out on the town with people in the same stage of life as you.

10. Be too busy to notice that you're single.

A number of my friends met their soul mates when they were so excited about their own endeavors that they hardly had time to schedule a date! Reconnect with the fabulous dreams and talents that you haven't tapped into recently. List three things you would love to do before you die, and pick one that you can complete in the next year. This focus will be great for you *and* for the men you meet—they will be drawn to your exciting life and will want to be a part of it. Men love a positive woman, and doing something you love will give you an instant boost.

When you're able to, be thankful for who and where you are. If you're like most Americans, chances are you'll get married one day. So—while you're single—take the time to focus on you and to celebrate the wonderful catch *you* are.

—

Acknowledgments

When one of my friends cried to me after she realized she was falling for a man whom she "did not mean to love," the idea for this book was born. Even through her tears, I knew that she had peace in her heart because she was following it.

Over the years, I have met numerous women who fell for unexpected partners and confirmed that once they got clearer on their love lists, and once they committed to breaking unhealthy dating patterns, their lives changed.

I don't believe in fear-based dating advice or the idea that there is something wrong with people simply because they are single. I dedicate this book to all the amazing singles out there who know in their hearts that someone is damn lucky to find them. Please don't settle for less than being the best version of yourself when you commit to a lifetime with one person. You deserve to be supported, expressed, cherished—and to find someone you absolutely adore (with no excuses).

Gratitude

Ever since I was a little girl, my mom, the English teacher, edited my stories. Before I handed in any school assignment, my mom marked up the pages and taught me how to write prose. Even when I couldn't string a sentence together (and trust me, I couldn't), my mom believed that I had a good writing voice and encouraged me to express it. She also happens to be the best mom in the world. For this reason, Marilyn Syrtash is the first person I want to thank in this book. I may not have been able to write a book if it weren't for her.

Nor could I have written anything remotely interesting or insightful if I had stayed in my own bubble and been satisfied with what lay in front of my eyes. My father, Peter Syrtash, opened the world to me. Literally. When I was growing up, he took me to faraway countries each year and encouraged me to keep exploring. He survived the Holocaust as a child in hiding, and he has always taught me the value of taking risks and working hard to reap rewards.

Finally, my sister, Veronica Syrtash, has been a huge support in my life, and she has been especially supportive since I signed my book contract. Veronica was able to zero in on themes and catch mistakes that I may have otherwise overlooked in the manuscript. She has a natural talent for writing and editing, and I have relied on her opinion throughout the writing process. She could have had a fabulous career as a professional editor if she had just quit her day job as a music lawyer. . . .

And while I'm talking about awesome editors, I must thank my amazingly patient, insightful, and talented editor at Rodale, Julie Will. Julie has always cleared time in her busy schedule to answer my questions and share great suggestions. When Julie initially heard my book proposal, I could tell that she *got it*, and I trusted her completely to help me execute the idea.

Rodale supports the idea of living well and living whole—I truly felt like we were a match the moment I walked in! Thank you to the whole team at Rodale, including Christina Gaugler,

Amy King, Nancy Bailey, Zachary Greenwald, and Yelena Nesbit, who have all worked hard to help support my book's vision.

I would not have sold this book, of course, if it weren't for my star literary agent, Ryan Fisher-Harbage. Ryan and I hit it off immediately, and he has been amazingly encouraging of my career. He has been a wonderful and creative source whenever I've wanted or needed to process ideas. Ryan has the ability to make things sound simple that I may otherwise obsess over! He is also one of the most relaxed and efficient agents I can imagine working with.

To my in-laws, who were the subject of my last book, thank you for your patience this past year and thank you for raising such a special NT. I'm so lucky to have you in my life.

Thank you to my family members—Muci, Aunt Dorothy and Uncle Al, Aunty Sally and Uncle Morris, Johnny and Miriam, and all my amazing cousins who celebrated my book deal with a fabulous *He's Just Not Your Type* cake (I'm guessing it was custom ordered).

For all my amazing friends who tolerated the months of sporadic e-mails and dodgy plans—thank you for your understanding and support these last few months. There are too many awesome friends to mention in Toronto, New York, the Bay Area, and Los Angeles—but you make my life much richer.

I especially want to thank my friends, and the amazing women I met along the way, who shared their unconventional love stories for *He's Just Not Your Type*. I also want to thank those who spoke so candidly about breaking up with seemingly perfect catches. To all of you who shared your experiences, I am incredibly grateful. Your stories helped shape this book and inspired me.

A big thank you to OkCupid.com, a fun, free dating site that conducted surveys on behalf of this book (OkCupid is the perfect site to use for my dating dares!), and to the Coaches Training Institute, which inspired some of the exercises I have included in the book.

I want to highlight a talented writer/editor and friend, Rebecca Raphael, whose feedback on the first few chapters fueled me to keep going. I must share gratitude for those amazing friends who gave me the space (that I so desperately craved!) to write in their beautiful homes. In particular, Janna Harowitz; Steve MacKay and his partner, Dan; and Mariana Roytman Schiffner and her husband, Dan Schiffner—your feedback on my work and your support mean so much.

Finally, how can I not thank my nontype, Michael? I literally could not have written this book if it weren't for him. He inspires me, challenges me, and supports me every day. For all the teasing I do in this book, and for all the times that I mention I was "horrified" to fall for someone like Michael, I hope he knows how incredibly lucky I feel that he picked me to marry, and how absolutely delighted I am with my choice to be his wife. In fact, being with him is the best decision I have ever made.

About the Author

Andrea Syrtash is a dating and relationship expert, life coach, and author. She has contributed to over a dozen relationship advice books and is the editor of *How to Survive the Real World* and *How to Survive Your In-Laws*. She is a regular advice columnist and contributor to numerous popular Web sites, including Oprah. com, Yahoo!, and the Huffington Post, and is the on-air host of *ON Dating*, produced by NBC Digital Studios. Andrea has shared advice in various media outlets across the country, including the *Today* show, VH1, *USA Today*, and NPR. She was recently the subject of an NHK Japan documentary about her work as a "love advisor." She is passionate about helping women live authentically—in life and in love. Andrea lives with her (nontype) husband in New York City. Visit Andrea at www.andreasyrtash.com.